STUDIES IN SOCIOLOGY

This series, prepared under the auspices of the British Sociological Association, is designed to provide short but comprehensive and scholarly treatments of key problem-areas in sociology. The books do not offer summary accounts of the current state of research in various fields, but seek rather to analyse matters which are the subject of controversy or debate. The series is designed to cover a broad range of topics, falling into three categories: (1) abstract problems of social theory and social philosophy; (2) interpretative questions posed by the writings of leading social theorists; (3) issues in empirical sociology. In addition, the series will carry translations of important writings in sociology which have not previously been available in English. Each book makes a substantive contribution to its particular topic, while at the same time giving the reader an indication of the main problems at issue; each carries an annotated bibliography, comprising a critical survey of relevant further literature.

ANTHONY GIDDENS

University of Cambridge

STUDIES IN SOCIOLOGY

General Editor: ANTHONY GIDDENS
Editorial Advisers: T. B. BOTTOMORE, DAVID LOCKWOOD and
ERNEST GELLNER

Published

THE SOCIOLOGY OF SOCIAL MOVEMENTS
J. A. Banks

POLITICS AND SOCIOLOGY IN THE THOUGHT OF MAX WEBER
Anthony Giddens

THE USE OF OFFICIAL STATISTICS IN SOCIOLOGY
Barry Hindess

STRIKES AND INDUSTRIAL CONFLICT: Britain and Scandinavia
Geoffrey K. Ingham

PROFESSIONS AND POWER
Terence J. Johnson

CONSCIOUSNESS AND ACTION AMONG THE WESTERN WORKING CLASS
Michael Mann

THE SOCIAL PROCESS OF INNOVATION: A STUDY IN THE SOCIOLOGY OF
SCIENCE
M. J. Mulkay

Forthcoming

KNOWLEDGE AND IDEOLOGY IN THE SOCIOLOGY OF EDUCATION
Gerald Bernbaum

MARXIST SOCIOLOGY
Tom Bottomore

POWER: A RADICAL VIEW
Steven Lukes

THE DEVELOPMENT OF THE SOCIOLOGY OF KNOWLEDGE
Steven Lukes

THE ORGANISATION OF CRIME
Mary McIntosh

CLASS THEORY AND THE DIVISION OF LABOUR
Gavin Mackenzie

MICHELS AND THE CRITIQUE OF SOCIAL DEMOCRACY
F. Parkin

Strikes and Industrial Conflict

Britain and Scandinavia

GEOFFREY K. INGHAM

Fellow of Christ's College and
University Assistant Lecturer in Sociology,
University of Cambridge

Macmillan

First published 1974 by
THE MACMILLAN PRESS LTD
London and Basingstoke
Associated companies in New York Dublin
Melbourne Johannesburg and Madras

SBN 333 13435 4

Printed in Great Britain by
THE ANCHOR PRESS LTD
Tiptree, Essex

CONTENTS

INTRODUCTION

THROUGHOUT the 1950s and 1960s it was fashionable for sociologists to conceptualise the changes in the structure of western industrial societies since the nineteenth century as a process of *institutionalisation*. It had been argued in the nineteenth century that capitalist industrialisation had transformed these societies in such a way that new classes and strata had emerged which rendered the traditional institutions obsolete and consequently inadequate for their task of regulating social divisions and conflicts. The analytical presentation of this observation was, in essence, common to many writers including, for example, Marx and de Tocqueville – despite their rather different evaluations of the process. For Marx, capitalist development had eroded the morally sanctioned bonds of feudal society and linked the new classes of bourgeoisie and proletariat by the stark cash nexus. Similarly, de Tocqueville pointed out the harshness of authority relations in a situation in which the masters had abrogated the responsibilities of paternalism while retaining its material privileges and the servants no longer saw obedience as a divine obligation. In other words, observers noted that the major economic and political conflicts were characterised by the absence of appropriate institutionalised normative regulation.

Encouraged by what they have taken to be empirical refutations of Marx's basic propositions regarding the demise of capitalist society, many sociologists have identified the major developments in twentieth-century western societies as those in which classes and strata have, through conflict, forged conciliatory institutions by which the instability and disorder of earlier capitalism has been overcome. The 'rules of the game', it is argued, have replaced physical force and naked economic domination as the means of resolving conflicts over the distribution of societies' scarce resources. So much so, that in 1959 a major proponent of this thesis could, in discussing the apparent diminution of ideological bitterness, argue quite candidly that :

> This change in western political life reflects the fact that the fundamental political problems of the industrial revolution have been solved. . . .[1]

For such writers the growth of political citizenship, the party system and elections represent a 'democratic translation of the class struggle' and relatedly the growth of trade unions, employers' associations and collective bargaining are seen as reducing the incidence and intensity of the basic class antagonism – that is, industrial conflict. In addition the absolute and steady increases in prosperity since the 1930s by means of rapidly accelerating G.N.P. and welfare measures appear to have met the basic material expectations of the working classes in western societies which, in turn, has facilitated both the viability and extension of the regulatory norms and institutions :

> Through industrial development under democratic auspices, the most important legitimately-to-be expected aspirations of the 'working class' have, in fact, been realized.[2]

In sharp contrast to Marxist theorising this particular interpretation of western industrial society sees no basic contradiction between economic and industrial infrastructures and the emerging superstructure of regulatory norms. Rather, industrial societies have basically *similar infrastructures* for which there are *appropriate* and *functional* institutions. Moreover, for the advocates of this thesis, the capitalist ruling classes appear not to impose the institutions and norms in order to control and manipulate the working classes; on the contrary, such writers as Lipset

[1] S. M. Lipset, *Political Man* (London, 1960) p. 406.
[2] Talcott Parsons, 'Communism and the West', in *Social Change*, ed. A. and E. Etzioni (Glencoe, Ill., 1964).

imply that capitalism as a system has the inherent capacity for self-regulation through the almost spontaneous emergence of institutions which serve the interests of *all* classes and, thus, 'genuinely' integrates the working class into society.

This school of thought sees manifest variations in the levels of institutionalisation between industrial societies as a consequence of diverse *cultural* and *historical* factors which are not intrinsic to capitalism as such but are features of the pre-industrial social order which are more entrenched in some societies than in others. In general Europe's feudal heritage and in particular the persistent religious and regional differentiation in continental Europe are held to explain the retarded growth of institutionalisation in contrast to Britain, Scandinavia and the United States. As Lipset stated as late as 1964 :

> one might argue that the absence of a traditional feudal past should mean that the United States has been most likely to develop the pure institutions of a capitalist industrial society . . . the social organization of the United States has presented the image of the European future.[3]

The present essay will be concerned with a critical analysis of one strand of the argument which deals with this general development; namely, the institutionalisation of industrial conflict. Our starting-point will be an examination of the major contribution in this field – Ross and Hartman's *Changing Patterns of Industrial Conflict*.[4] Here it is forcefully argued on the basis of comparative sociological and statistical analyses that 'the strike has been going out of style' or 'withering away'. By way of a close inspection of their work and the introduction of more recent and different statistical evidence I hope to show that Ross and Hartman's conclusions are in need of significant modification. The major part of the essay comprises an analysis of the development of the institutions of collective bargaining in Britain, Sweden,

[3] S. M. Lipset, 'The Changing Class Structure and Contemporary European Politics', *Daedalus* (Winter 1964) p. 272.

[4] Ross and Hartman [16] (Publication details are cited in the Bibliography, pp. 93–4.)

Norway and Denmark. The choice of societies is by no means arbitrary. The authors of *Changing Patterns* grouped these countries together as those in which the process of institutionalisation and subsequent 'withering' of the strike had proceeded farthest. However, by drawing what I consider to be a relatively sharp contrast between Britain and Scandinavia I hope to illustrate the complexities of a process many writers have tended to over-simplify. More specifically, an attempt will be made to account, in general terms, for observed variations in the levels of institutionalisation by reference to important differences in the *industrial infrastructures* of the societies in question. The specific way in which the concept of infrastructure is used will be dealt with in Chapter 3; but, in general terms, it is meant to refer to those features of a society's economic and technological system which shape the organisation of, and the social relationships between, those groups engaged in the process of production. Conflicts between these groups – that is, between unions and employers – produce, in turn, the institutions of normative regulation. To take one example, I will argue that variations between societies in their degree of economic competition at certain crucial stages of industrialisation are related to differences in both the structure of employers' associations and the system of institutional regulation.

The present essay is not meant to be a general introductory text on industrial conflict in all its forms; but rather an introduction to some basic issues in the sociology of industrial relations via an examination of a single and relatively narrow problem. In an essay of this length the treatment of many problems is inevitably sketchy and brief. What follows is therefore tentative but, hopefully, capable of being extended and supported.

1. THE ROSS AND HARTMAN THESIS

ROSS and Hartman assert that the trend towards the withering away of the strike has, on the whole, been most pronounced in Northern Europe; but is also evident to a lesser degree in North America. The main evidence for this conclusion is contained in the two tables below which show: (1) the percentage of union members involved in strikes over three periods of time from 1900 to 1956, and (2) a comparison of the average duration of strikes in the periods 1900–29 and 1948–56. The tables are taken directly from Ross and Hartman; but only include those countries in which the decline in strike activity has been most marked.

The authors did, in fact, have four other measures of strike activity; but concluded that:

We have found, however, that distinctive patterns of industrial conflict can be described most intelligently in terms of the membership involvement ratio (percentage of union members going on strike) and the duration of strikes (days lost per striker) ([16] p. 12).

TABLE I *Percentage of union membership involved in strikes*

	1900–29	1930–47	1948–56
Denmark	6·3	2·4	1·4
Netherlands	7·0	2·6	1·3
United Kingdom	16·1	6·4	5·9
Norway	27·0	6·8	1·2
Sweden	22·7	3·0	0·3
United States	33·2	20·3	15·4
Canada	14·7	13·3	6·3

Source: [16] p. 18.

11

TABLE 2   Average duration of strikes $\dfrac{(working\ days\ lost)}{(number\ of\ strikers)}$

	1900–29	1948–56	1948–56 as a percentage of 1900–29
Denmark	28·7	4·3	15
Netherlands	32·7	7·5	23
United Kingdom	23·0	4·3	19
Norway	33·6	15·2	45
Sweden	37·1	22·6	61
United States	statistics for 1900–29 not available		
Canada	27·1	19·3	71

Source: [16] p. 24.

Before passing on to a brief summary of the explanation Ross and Hartman give for their findings, it is important to note several criticisms of the way in which they handled their strike data. The first point one notices about Tables 1 and 2 is the wide differences in the spans of time which constitute the periods by which the data are classified: 1900–29 – thirty years; 1930–47 – eighteen years; and 1948–56 – nine years. No reason is given for this procedure : the demarcations seem at first glance to be purely arbitrary. But if this were the case one may legitimately ask why the periods were not more uniform in size. In fact, the full strike data presented in Ross and Hartman's Appendix are capable of being presented in a way which does not show such a startling and uniform decline. For example, in the case of Great Britain the decline in the percentage of union members going on strike occurred in the early 1920s and no clear pattern can be discerned since that time. The United States is even more difficult to fit into Ross and Hartman's generalisation. After the very early decline in union members taking strike action the pattern is extremely variable : several periods, especially during the 1920s, show lower membership activity than the latest 1948–56 period. Canada shows a similar pattern to the United States when scrutinised closely. Only the Scandinavian countries – Sweden, Norway and Denmark – plus the Netherlands show a decline in union

12

members going on strike which is both very marked and a clear and uniform trend. To be sure, Ross and Hartman do note that the withering process is less marked in North America; but they include Great Britain with the Scandinavian societies and also refer to a 'general decline in strike activity throughout much of the industrialised world'. The average duration of strikes shows an even more variable pattern, which Ross and Hartman in fact acknowledge. Moreover, by comparing the latest short nine-year period (1948–56) with the long earliest period of thirty years (1900–29) the authors undoubtedly exaggerate the trend they identified. For example, in another table they show the average duration of strikes in the form of averages for nineteen three-year periods and these data show quite distinctly that in Sweden a real decline in duration can only be discerned unambiguously in the very short post-1948 period. ([16] p. 26) Therefore, even on the basis of their own measures, it would seem that Ross and Hartman tend to exaggerate the extent of the general process of the withering away of the strike and consequently fail to note that the process is only clearly apparent in the Scandinavian societies and the Netherlands. Moreover, *Changing Patterns* does not make use of a measure of strike activity which is to be found in almost all other studies of this kind; namely, strike *frequency* (i.e. *number* of strikes per *n*. workers).[1] And, as we shall see in Chapter 2, the use of this particular measure allows an even sharper distinction to be made between the Scandinavian societies and Great Britain. In other words, Britain's strike pattern over time in terms of the number of strikes will be seen to be much nearer those of France and the United States than the northern European countries with which Ross and Hartman place it.

The attempt to explain the findings as presented in *Changing Patterns* has much to commend it. The work is widely comparative, and, in contrast to much writing in the field of industrial relations, takes the view that 'the industrial-relations system in any country is part of a larger social context'. ([16] p. 173)

---

[1] The number of disputes is presented in Table A–1 of the Appendix to Ross and Hartman; but, strangely, these data are not used in any systematic way.

In other words, Ross and Hartman attempt a structural analysis of the societies in question. When isolating certain factors as 'conducive to industrial peace' they emphasise that their 'influence is executed jointly rather than severally, as a *configuration* rather than as a group of *independent* variables'. ([16] p. 174, italic mine)

The actual presentation of the explanations of their basic findings is, however, slightly confusing. In chapter 5 it is stated that:

In our opinion there are three primary reasons why the strike has been going out of style. First, employers have developed more sophisticated policies and more effective organisations. Second, the state has become more prominent as an employer of labor, economic planner, provider of benefits, and supervisor of industrial relations. Third, in many countries (although not in the United States) the labor movement has been forsaking the use of the strike in favor of broad political en-endeavours. ([16] p. 42)

Additionally, in this chapter, Ross and Hartman speculate that:

It may well be that rank and file members are not so predisposed towards strikes as they formerly were. ([16] p. 48)

However, after presenting the 'primary reasons' the authors, in the following chapter, add three other very closely related 'influences' on strike activity comprising what amounts to a fifth factor which assumes great importance in their subsequent analysis.[2] They refer to the integration and maturity of the labour movement and the consolidation of mutually recognised union-

[2] [16] pp. 63–4. The three 'influences' are: 1. *Organisational stability:* (a) Age of the labour movement; (b) Stability of membership in recent years. 2. *Leadership conflicts* in the labour movement: (a) Factionalism, rival unionism and rival federations; (b) Strength of communism in labour unions. 3. *Status of union-management relations:* (a) Degree of acceptance by employers; (b) Consolidation of bargaining structure.

14

management relations – in other words, the emergence of stable institutions for the regulation of industrial relations.

First, employers are seen as having gradually changed their attitudes to the employment relationship. Ross and Hartman quote, approvingly, Lester's contention that :

the pre-World War I 'commodity concept' of employment has been displaced by a post-World War II 'welfare concept' of employer–employee relations.[3]

That is to say, one major reason for the decline in strike activity is the increasing tolerance and reasonableness of employers. This change of attitude is embodied in the institutions of mature systems of collective bargaining and apparent in the 'interesting personality changes' in the type of men chosen for top positions in industry. 'Buccaneering railroad magnates of the nineteenth century' and 'highbinding bankers and brokers of the 1920s' have given way to 'a tamer, soberer and less imaginative generation' in which labour relations managers have become 'less excited about fundamental principles and more interested in practical results, more conciliatory'. ([16] p. 48) But as an explanation of their problem, the above comments are far too superficial; they describe certain aspects of the institutionalisation of industrial conflict rather than explain the process. Basically, Ross and Hartman fail to note that the differences between their caricatures of the nineteenth-century capitalist and his twentieth-century successor are not merely a consequence of what they conceptualise as personality changes. Rather, what may be more adequately termed changes in orientation toward industrial relations are themselves closely related to fundamental changes in the structure of capitalist business enterprises. During the same period in which organised labour of western industrial societies was demanding recognition and the acceptance of some form of collective bargaining the large-scale, bureaucratised joint-stock company was becoming more prevalent. And, as Bendix has pointed out, the legitimation of the new *managerial* stratum's control could not

[3] Richard A. Lester, 'Revolution in Industrial Employment', *Labor Law Journal*, 9 (1958) cited in [16] p. 47.

be effected with reference to the *entrepreneurial* ideology of rugged individualism and the self-evident superiority of one who had struggled competitively to become a successful owner of property.[4] Rather, the managerial claim for the legitimation of their control is based upon their supposed ability to efficiently administer and co-ordinate highly complex social and technical organisations. Thus, the shift from the 'commodity' to the 'welfare' concept of labour must be seen as an *ideological* change and, as such, it may be noted in addition that one must be wary of inferring any direct and completely commensurate change in *actual* actions on the part of those who own and control industry.

The development of the modern state, according to Ross and Hartman, has influenced the decline of strike activity in four basic ways. First, in nationalised industries conflict is more likely to be resolved politically and this reduces the likelihood of a protracted trial of economic strength. Second, 'where the state plays an active role in economic planning, it has a strong motive to ensure that its plans are not frustrated'. ([16] p. 50) Third, 'through protective legislation and social security programs, the state disposes of issues that might otherwise be the focus of labor-management conflict'. ([16] p. 50) Fourth, for the above and other reasons the state, to varying degrees in the countries in question, has taken upon itself the important role of conciliator or arbitrator. Of course, it is most plausible that, given the existence of a withering of the strike, the state's role in the process could be of the kind outlined by Ross and Hartman. However, as with all their assertions no direct evidence is presented to show that the state's involvement has been one of the primary and basic factors in the reduction of strike activity. For example, there is little to suggest that, in any society, nationalised industries are less strike-prone than private ones. On the contrary, the existence of a single clearly identifiable employer (the state) may often act as a stimulus to previously highly differentiated, dispersed and unorganised occupational groups who may be consequently involved in protracted strikes which might not have arisen in the absence of such

[4] Reinhard Bendix, *Work and Authority in Industry* (New York, 1956).

16

a central focus for their grievances. For example, public employees were involved in long and intense strikes during the 1960s in those western societies where inflation caused governments to impose wage controls particularly in those sectors where they had most chance of success; that is to say, with their own employees. In short, Ross and Hartmann's arguments with respect to the state are no more than plausible and, moreover, it is clear that government intervention in industry can, under a wide variety of conditions, encourage workers to unionise and also stimulate strike action.

Finally, they argue that the actions of working-class-based political parties, especially when they have formed governments as in the case of several northern European countries, have enabled workers to gain their objectives without sacrificing income. This particular argument has been formulated in a more precise and sophisticated way by Dahrendorf, who refers to the 'institutional isolation' of industrial conflict in western society and the way in which this has led to a reduction of its intensity and violence. By this is not meant that relationships between the polity and economy have become more attenuated : on the contrary, Dahrendorf, in common with others, points to the increasingly close association of the two spheres. Rather, Dahrendorf sees the development of specialised and relatively autonomous institutions for dealing with industrial conflict. To be sure, it must be stressed that the autonomy of the institutions of collective bargaining is relative in a very real sense; but Dahrendorf wishes primarily to contrast the situation in the twentieth century with that of the earlier period when political and industrial grievances were *superimposed* and thereby more intense in societies characterised by the absence of structural arrangements for the resolution of class conflicts.[5]

Ross and Hartman's assertions concerning the effects of working-class political action are more closely related to their speculative proposals that workers' motivations to strike have weakened than they are to Dahrendorf's theories. They register strong agreement, albeit in an unsystematic way, with the ortho-

[5] Ralf Dahrendorf [2] pp. 267–79.

doxy of the 1950s in which many writers maintained that the working classes had been integrated into advanced industrial societies both economically and politically. A year later than Lipset in *Political Man*, Ross and Hartman argued in a similar vein that the increasing affluence and economic planning of industrial societies had satisfied workers' economic wants, relieved them of the insecurities of the pre-Keynesian economies and thus formed a sound material basis for the already existing political integration brought about by the extension of citizenship. Thus, they argued, political action from the workers' point of view, is more 'dignified and respectable' and 'more in line with the middle-class orientation of workers in advanced industrial society'. Although it is never spelled out in a concise manner, Ross and Hartman, following R. A. Lester, clearly attach much importance to the *embourgeoisement* of the working classes in reducing strike activity. A decline in economic inequality, it was argued, by way of general affluence, progressive income-tax and other state measures and a reduction of social distance between the classes has produced workers 'with middle-class mores and living standards who resist any extended interruption of income' which in turn has meant that 'class antagonisms and spontaneous inclinations to strike have declined'. ([16] p. 45) Since Ross and Hartman wrote these lines a large literature has become available on the class structure of western societies in general and the hypothesised *embourgeoisement* of the working class in particular. For the moment it is only necessary to say that this has led to a modification, in three important respects, of the kind of views held in the 1950s. First, the earlier pronouncements concerning the decline of economic inequality in western industrial societies have been shown to be overoptimistic. Second, by way of a closer examination and application of the classic writings of Marx and Weber on social stratification it is now generally recognised as theoretically unsound to conceptualise class merely in terms of level of income and/or style of life. In determining class position, greater emphasis is now given to the structured location of groups and individuals in the labour and commodity markets : in short, an increase in income does not in itself change one's class. Third, it can now be seen – as it should have been

18

from the outset – that an improvement in the material standards of life for the working classes does not permanently inhibit their economic grievances and pecuniary expectations.

As I have pointed out, after discussing in chapter 5 of their book what they consider to be the 'primary' reasons for the withering away of the strike, Ross and Hartman add three more factors in the following chapter which may be viewed together as the *institutionalisation* of industrial relations and industrial conflict. First, they suggest that the age and maturity of the labour movement have an effect on industrial conflict :

> older movements are more likely to have completed their struggles for existence, recognition, and security, and to be integrated into their national economies. Once this point has been reached, bargaining machinery can be developed to handle economic issues without frequent work stoppages. ([16] p. 65)

Second, they argue that factionalism and rival leadership in trade unions exacerbate industrial conflict in so far as the different groups may compete with each other in pressing claims and calling strikes. And conversely :

> The union structure most conducive to the elimination of industrial conflict is a unified national movement with strongly centralized control. ([16] p. 66)

The third 'influence' outlined in chapter 6 overlaps to a great extent with many of the assertions already made. That is to say, Ross and Hartman state quite simply that the acceptance of unionism and collective bargaining by the employers and the growth of relatively centralised bargaining are 'conducive to industrial peace'.

In the most general terms the thesis of the institutionalisation of industrial conflict is, I believe, incontestable. The development of procedural norms for the regulation of conflict between employers and workers will reduce the incidence of strike activity for the simple reason that the withdrawal of labour (or an employer's lock-out) no longer constitutes the primary means for settling a dispute. There are, however, certain problematic implications of this almost truistic assertion. In the first place, Ross and Hartman, for reasons which will be dealt with in some detail later, are most certainly overenthusiastic in stating that the institutionalisation of industrial conflict through collective bargaining involves 'the virtual elimination of the strike'. Second, it is never completely clear whether Ross and Hartman consider that the expression of industrial or class conflict in the form of strikes is diminished by this process of institutionalisation and consequently takes on other forms, such as 'working-to-rule' or industrial sabotage, or that the basic conflictual nature of the employment relationship in capitalist society is overcome or removed. In all fairness, Ross and Hartman do note that it is not essential to their argument that 'the strike has been going out of style' to state that worker dissatisfaction has decreased. But, as we have seen, they strongly imply that affluence, government welfare and other measures and the growth of working-class political activity have qualitatively changed class relationships to the extent that the basic, if at times latent, conflict between classes has actually diminished. Nowhere do they consider the idea that if the distribution of scarce material resources remains unequal and is to a large extent a consequence of relatively 'unprincipled' bargaining in the 'market-place'; and if the work situation and life chances of the large majority are controlled by a minority of materially more privileged individuals then the social relationships of such a system will be inherently and objectively marked by conflict. Perhaps more important is that Ross and Hartman do not notice the theoretical implications of their speculative proposals about the decline in workers' inherent propensity to strike. If affluence and the satisfaction of virtually all economic expectations had, in fact, substantially reduced basic industrial militancy this would be *in itself* a sufficient explanation of the withering away of the strike. The institutionalisation of industrial relations would, if their secondary argument were in any way correct, become increasingly redundant. But along with many sociologists of the 1950s Ross and Hartman seemed unaware of the Marxist argument that the continual extension and modification of regulatory institutions testify to the persistence of structured conflict in capitalist societies.[6]

Most of the problems with Ross and Hartman's approach stem, I believe, directly from the unsatisfactory nature of their explanation of this process of institutionalisation. There is a strong implication that the emergence of regulatory norms and institutions is 'natural' and spontaneous: in other words they intimate that whenever organised groups engage in frequent conflict over a sufficiently long period of time they almost inevitably find 'ways and means of living together'. Like their basic assertion that the institutionalisation of industrial conflict involves a reduction of strike activity, such conclusions are an oversimplification and I would contend that a conceptualisation of the institutionalisation of industrial conflict as a self-regulatory process inhibits the understanding of very important issues. Ross and Hartman are unable to deal adequately with two crucial problems; namely: (i) the explanation of variations in levels of institutionalisation between societies which cannot be accounted for merely by differences in the age of the labour movement and (ii) the possibility of a breakdown of the normative regulation of industrial conflict. It is significant that in their attempts to explain important variations in the degree of formalisation and centralisation of collective bargaining Ross and Hartman have recourse to factors which are external to their basic theoretical system. What may be termed 'culture' and 'personality' variables are introduced into their argument in a most unsystematic way. In contrasting the overall levels of institutionalisation between countries in which capital and labour have been at least minimally organised for a similiar length of time they state that:

[6] David Lockwood, 'Some Remarks on the Social System', *British Journal of Sociology*, vii (1956) 134–43. '. . . the presence of a normative order, or common value system, does not mean that conflict has disappeared, or been resolved in some way, instead, the very existence of a normative order mirrors the continual potentiality of conflict'. This argument is, of course, essentially similar to that which is found in Marx's critique of Hegel, who had argued that the state in various ways successfully harmonises the conflicts and divisions of 'civil society'.

we may confidently state that the willingness to 'muddle through' is unevenly distributed over the globe. For example, the graceful retreat of the English from India and Burma may be contrasted with the debacles suffered by the French in Indo-China and Algeria. ([16] p. 174)

Similarly, the 'unity and centralisation' in the labour movements of Scandinavia and the United Kingdom and the 'rivalry and disorganisation' in those of France and Italy are related to what are called 'differences in national "style" and culture' which produce the 'stolid, practical Englishman or Scandinavian and the excitable, individualistic Frenchman or Italian'. ([16] p. 174) Not only is such theorising *ad hoc* in the present context, but it is also generally tautologous: stolid practical Englishmen appear to be at one and the same time evidence for and a result of English national 'style' and culture.[7] A further general implication of this kind of analysis, and one which I will return to in the concluding chapter, is that industrial societies possess such similar industrial infrastructures that variations in their normative and institutional arrangements must be explained by reference to culture, values or the intrusion of unique historical events.[8]

A more adequate interpretation of the overall process of institutionalisation and, consequently, a more satisfactory explanation of variations in (i) the levels of institutionalisation and (ii) the degree of centralisation of collective bargaining can best be achieved by taking into account the nature of societies' industrial systems at various stages in their development.

It is, I believe, unhelpful even to imply that a *modus vivendi* is a spontaneous and almost inevitable consequence of conflict between organised groups. Rather, the specific nature of the power struggles between employers, workers and the state must

[7] For a criticism of this kind of theorising see J. Blake and K. Davies, 'Norms, Values and Sanctions', in *Handbook of Modern Sociology*, ed. R. E. L. Faris (Chicago, 1967).

[8] As I pointed out in the Introduction this 'metatheory' marks the work of many writers during the 1950s and early 1960s. See especially the work of S. M. Lipset, *Political Man* (New York, 1960), and *First New Nation* (New York, 1963).

be located in the infrastructures in which they take place and from which the conflicting parties gain their relative organisational and economic strengths. To say, without little further comment that norms 'emerge' and are consistent with the prevalent common values is scarcely illuminating. More often than not, regulatory norms and institutions are imposed by those with superior power – that is, in the present context by the industrial bourgeoisie or the state. To be sure, the specific content of norms and institutions may be *understood* within the context of existing values and cultural traditions; but the problems of how and why the institutions came into being cannot be *explained* by reference to these factors alone. In the subsequent analysis of Scandinavia and Great Britain I will argue that an account of the different roles played by the employers in these countries is crucial in explaining variations in their respective systems of industrial relations. Furthermore, the varying roles of employers can, I believe be related quite closely to long-standing and significant differences in the industrial structures of the societies in question. In short, then, the major part of the paper will be devoted to an analysis of the relationship between industrial infrastructure and the overall level of institutionalisation and degree of centralisation of the systems of industrial relations in Britain and Scandinavia.

In addition, if one views economic activity in society as involving a continual transformation of the means of production then the possibility of emerging contradictions between a changing infrastructure and institutions forged in an earlier period can clearly be seen. This commonplace Marxian insight is conspicuously absent from that body of thought in the 1950s and early 1960s which argued that the fundamental problems of the industrial revolution had been solved and also from Ross and Hartman's *Changing Patterns of Industrial Conflict*, which, I have tried to argue, can be placed firmly within this school.[9]

[9] The 'school' could, of course, be physically as well as intellectually located – that is, on the Berkeley campus of the University of California.

2. PATTERNS OF STRIKE ACTIVITY

THIS chapter is mainly concerned with an assessment of Ross and Hartman's conclusions in the light of more recent data and different measures of strike activity. As I have stated, Britain and Scandinavia will be the major focus of interest, but strike statistics from the United States and France will also be presented initially in order to place the former societies in a wider comparative perspective. The first task, however, is to outline briefly some of the persistent and seemingly intractable methodological problems which face the student of industrial conflict.

Most studies of variations in strike rates contain some kind of assumption which relates the measures of strike activity to the incidence, pervasiveness or severity of industrial conflict. Strikes are taken as unambiguous indicators or 'operational definitions' of conflict. However, as some writers have noted, although strikes may be taken to denote the existence of conflict the absence of strikes does not necessarily signify an absence of conflict. In other words, strikes are but one of many possible expressions of industrial conflict. Workers use many sanctions and strategies in pursuit of their goals : machine-breaking during early industralisation has been termed 'collective bargaining by riot',[1] and, in the bureaucratised organisations of advanced industrial society, 'working-to-rule' has often proved as effective as a complete withdrawal of labour. It has also been argued that conflict may be measured by individual as well as collective action. For example, 'industrial sabotage may be an important index of underlying

[1] Eric Hobsbawm, 'The Machine Breakers' in *Labouring Men: Studies in the History of Labour* (London, 1964).

industrial conflict'[2] and in a recent study of the Swedish car industry, which the authors characterise as having relatively few strikes but a high rate of labour turnover, it is asserted that 'an unusually rational system of collective organisation has driven the less articulate forms of discontent into individual modes of expression'.[3]

Despite the need for a general study of the various modes of expressing conflict in industry, the present work is concerned with the narrower issue of the relationship between the institutionalisation of industrial conflict and strike action. However, this limitation of scope does not, unfortunately, mean that the conceptual and methodological problems are significantly reduced. There are, in fact, two persistent problems in the measurement and use of comparative strike data.

First, there are some important variations between societies concerning the point at which a withdrawal of labour becomes officially classified as a strike. For example, British statistics exclude disputes not concerned with 'terms of employment or conditions of labour' and those involving less than ten workers or those lasting less than one day unless a loss of more than 100 days is involved. Norway, however, merely excludes disputes lasting less than one day and it would appear that the Swedes do not publish their criteria for defining a 'strike'. Clearly, if more societies presented detailed strike statistics broken down by the duration of individual strikes then this particular problem could be partially overcome.

However, the greatest difficulties stem from another source of variation in the definition and classification of strikes. There is now much evidence to confirm the frequent assertion that very many withdrawals of labour never pass through the process of being defined as a strike and, moreover, that this may occur in some societies to a greater extent than in others. For example, Kuhn's work on American industry shows that few firms kept statistics on 'unofficial' walkouts and that the management in one company

[2] L. Taylor and P. Walton, 'Industrial Sabotage' in *Images of Deviance*, ed. S. Cohen (Harmondsworth: Penguin Books, 1971).

[3] H. A. Turner *et al.*, *Labour Relations in the Motor Industry* (London, 1967) p. 131.

consistently reported about twice as many stoppages as the local union.[4] The most startling example of this problem comes from some recent trade union sponsored research in Sweden.[5] It is esti- mated that only about half the unofficial strikes which actually occur are reported to the employers' association and thence to the unions. Furthermore, even if unofficial strikes are reported to the employers and unions they do not necessarily find their way into the official statistics of the Swedish *Statistisk Arsbôk*. Be- tween 1960 and 1969 the number of unofficial strikes reported to the unions from the metal-working industry alone exceeded that presented by the government for the whole of Sweden. How- ever, it would be misleading to see such findings as the results of random errors in perception or faulty methodology on the part of those involved in collecting the official strike data. The social nature of the process of defining and classifying strikes means that the statistics provided by those parties directly involved are linked in a systematic way to their goals, strategies and relative positions of power. What may be tentatively termed the 'under- reporting' of strikes is likely to occur in quite varied circumstances. In general the hasty definition of a work stoppage as a strike may often prove a barrier to negotiations and a resumption of work. Many managers are likely to concur with the remark made by a foreman in Kuhn's study when referring to 'wildcat strikes' : 'As long as I get enough production, I'll take the nuisance'. In par- ticular, a native management in a company controlled by foreign capital may conceal labour 'troubles' through fear of outside en- croachments on their prerogative. In the Swedish case additional factors are involved in the obvious under-reporting. In the first place, strikes called during the term of an officially negotiated agreement are illegal and must be referred to the Labour Court and it seems that the system would become increasingly unwork- able if all unofficial disputes were reported. Second, it is also pos- sible that all groups in Swedish industry are reluctant to tarnish their image of having exceptionally 'peaceful' industrial relations.

The classification as strikes of almost all work stoppages, how-

[4] J. W. Kuhn, *Bargaining in Grievance Settlement* (New York, 1961).
[5] Walter Korpi, *Vilda Strejker inom Metall-och Verkstadsindustrien*, cited in Fulcher [7].

ever short, probably occurs less frequently; but there are situations in which some groups' interests may be served by the existence of a high strike rate. A zealous classification of work stoppages as strikes can clearly be a means of drawing attention to the existence of an industrial relations problem which requires corrective legislation. Or, in the early stages of unionisation competing branches of the labour movement may boast a high rate of successful strikes in order to attract new members.

Such a diversity of definitions and classifications of strikes makes international comparison a hazardous procedure. However, the recognition of the problem in the way I have briefly outlined it gives rise to another potentially useful area of study. That is to say, the social processes of defining and reporting strikes are themselves data which require explanation and an examination of variations in these processes may tell us as much about the social structures of various societies and industries as the more conventional analysis of the official figures.

Our second source of difficulty stems from the fact that strikes have a number of dimensions and therefore may be measured in a variety of ways each of which tells us something rather different about strike activity. As we have seen, Ross and Hartman developed six measures, but used only two : (i) the membership involvement ratio (percentage of union members going on strike), and (ii) the duration of strikes (days lost per striker). However, the most commonly used measures of strike activity are : (i) the duration of strikes – i.e. days lost per strike; (ii) size of strikes – i.e. strikers per strike; (iii) frequency of strikers – i.e. strikes per 100,000 workers; and (iv) total man days lost through strikes.

The present study will make use of only two measures : strike frequency and days lost. Both measures are expressed as a rate in order to facilitate comparative analysis. The duration of strikes measure is not used for several reasons. First, the raw strike data are in many cases only available in a form which permits the calculation of the *average* duration of strikes by the division of the total number of days lost by the total number of disputes. This is, however, not very instructive due to the extremely distorting effect the occurrence of one or two very large or long strikes can have. *Median* duration would clearly be more useful; but as I pointed out the data often do not exist for this calculation to be made. Second, the duration of strikes is not as directly related to our central problem as are the other two measures. In assessing the extent to which procedural norms replace strikes as the means of resolving industrial disputes the measure omitted by Ross and Hartman – strike frequency – is possibly most important. This measure expresses, albeit imperfectly, the willingness of workers to use strike action; whereas duration, as we shall see later, is more useful in indicating the relative power positions of capital and labour.[6]

In our reassessment of the 'withering away' thesis we may begin by looking at the days lost per 100,000 workers: these data are shown in Table 3.

The Scandinavian societies show a clear post Second World War decline in the number of days lost; but in Great Britain the decline is less marked. The figures for the United States, starting as they do as late as 1928, are really an inadequate basis for any sound generalisation; but, if anything, they show a general rise in the days lost through strike activity since the Second World War. In France the situation is less clear: a decline in days lost can be discerned until the events of 1968, since when strike activity has been at a high level. Of course, these findings support Ross and Hartman's basic conclusion. However there is an important qualification to be made; that is, the number of days lost per 100,000 workers in Great Britain is such that we cannot follow Ross and Hartman in placing Britain with the Scandinavian societies. This assertion receives greater support from our second measure – strike frequency (Table 4): only the Scandinavian societies show a decline in the number of disputes per 100,000

[6] The relationship between the *number* and *duration* of strikes is a complex one. For statistical and sociological reasons an inverse relationship can sometimes be discerned between the two measures. In the first place, the existence, in any given year, of very large and long strikes reduces the chances of the occurrence of a large number of small short ones. Second, workers are, understandably, often unwilling to strike again shortly after a long dispute.

TABLE 3 DAYS LOST IN DISPUTE (*in thousands*) *per 100,000 non-agricultural workers, expressed as four-year averages, from earliest date available to 1969*

	Great Britain	Sweden	Norway	Denmark	France	United States
1896–9	54					
1900–3	21			27	39	
1904–7	13	71	26	44	59	
1908–11	54	237	94	35	41	
1912–15	105	20	49	20	20	
1916–19	74	74	71	53	51	
1920–3	215	257	225	161	118	
1924–7	247	81	293	137	30	
1928–31	32	123	322	13	53	23
1932–5	16	102	45	7	18	63
1936–9	10	30	98	69	n.a.	57
1946–9	11	3	9·5	42	108	139
1950–3	8·5	10	6·8	0·3	62	78
1954–7	20	2	31	21	21	50
1958–61	17	0·5	12	46	13	61
1962–5	14	0·5	7	5·7	19	34
1966–9	19	3·4	0·9	3·7	19*	59

* Three years only.

workers. Here the trend observed by Ross and Hartman as far as 1956 can clearly be seen to have continued. The French and American figures show a slight rise since the Second World War; but in Great Britain, as most of us are already aware, a very marked increase in the number of disputes has occurred. As others have pointed out, with respect to the number of disputes the term 'flourishing' would be more apt than 'withering' when describing Britain's recent strike record ([4] p. 40).

Thus, the additional strike data from 1956 onwards and the use of different measures do not lead to any modification of the Ross and Hartman findings as far as Scandinavia is concerned. From the date when data are available until the 1930s these societies were characterised by a very high level of strike activity.

TABLE 4 STRIKE FREQUENCY: *number of disputes per 100,000 non-agricultural workers, expressed as four-year averages, from earliest date available to 1969 plus 1970*

	Great Britain	Sweden	Norway	Denmark	France	United States
1888–91	6·5					
1892–5	5·2					
1896–9	5·4					
1900–3	3·5			16·6	7·7	
1904–7	2·9	18·4		17·7	13·3	
1908–11	3·6	10·1		13·6	14·7	
1912–15	6·4	6·5		11·0	8·6	4·9*
1916–19	5·8	25·6		39·2	10·2	13·3
1920–3	5·3	19·8	9·0*	14·5	11·0	7·3
1924–7	2·8	12·2	11·5	5·2	10·7	3·6
1928–31	2·4	11·0	11·9	2·6	9·0	2·5
1932–5	2·7	6·5	14·2	2·5	3·7	6·3
1936–9	5·0	2·7	24·5	1·5	18·7	10·3
1946–9	9·3	2·7	5·2	2·6	13·7	9·1
1950–3	8·3	0·8	4·3	0·9	19·8	10·4
1954–7	12·1	0·7	2·4	2·8	20·1	7·5
1958–61	11·9	0·5	1·5	2·9	10·8	6·7
1962–5	10·7	0·5	0·6	2·3	13·9	6·3
1966–9	10·8	0·4	0·5	2·0	11·5*	7·4
1970	17·7	3·7	1·2	5·7	20·7	7·9

* Three years only.

Sources: The strike and labour force data used in Tables 3 and 4 are taken, in general, from various editions of the *Yearbook of Labour Statistics* (Geneva: International Labour Office, 1927–   ) and from the following sources for particular countries:

Great Britain: *Annual Abstract of Statistics* (London, 1911–   ); *Abstract of Labour Statistics, 1922–36* (London, 1937); *Report on Strikes and Lockouts*, Board of Trade, Department of Labour Statistics (London, 1894–1913); G. Routh, *Occupation and Pay in Great Britain, 1906–1966* (London: Cambridge University Press, 1965).

Sweden, Denmark and Norway: *Yearbook of Nordic Statistics* (Stockholm: The Nordic Council, various years).

In terms of the number of days lost the situation was very similar to that in Great Britain; but strike frequency was considerably higher. In other words, not only did Scandinavia experience large-scale protracted disputes as did Britain in this period, but also the incidence of a very large number of shorter strikes. Since that time strike frequency has declined very dramatically as has the number of days lost. Thus, on the basis of the tables, we must concur with Ross and Hartman and describe the contemporary strike pattern in Scandinavia as one in which there are relatively spasmodic and infrequent strikes which are of comparatively long duration. However, some qualifications must be made. As we noted earlier, a large number of short and unofficial strikes go unreported in Sweden and also possibly in the other Scandinavian societies given that they have similar systems of industrial relations. The discoverer of this state of affairs tried to put his new Swedish data in perspective by comparing them with the British figures and only counting those strikes which fell within the official British classification. This procedure revealed that the incidence of strikes in the British engineering industry was *twenty* times higher than that in the comparable Swedish industries. Fulcher, who reports this Swedish work, speculates that the method of comparison still tends to overemphasise the Anglo-Swedish differences in strike frequency.[7] However, all the available evidence points to the fact that the incidence of strikes in the Scandinavian countries is extremely low by international standards.

With respect to Great Britain we can agree with Ross and Hartman that large-scale protracted strikes, after reaching a peak during the 1920s, tended to become a rarity immediately after

[7] Fulcher [7]. His reasons are: (i) The cumbersome disputes procedure in Great Britain may mean that the 'short' strikes are longer in this country than in Sweden and consequently more strikes may fall outside the British definitional threshold in Sweden than is the case in Britain; (ii) evidence suggests that British employers are more avid recorders of disputes than their Swedish counterparts. The arguments are extremely speculative and they must be evaluated in light of the fact that Fulcher is at pains to minimise the differences between Sweden and Britain.

the Second World War. Although Ross and Hartman made no use of the strike-frequency measure, and consequently failed to note its rapid rise since the Second World War, they did, in fact, refer in their text to the persistence of a number of short 'unofficial strikes' in Great Britain. However, in their desire to classify Britain with Scandinavia they completely misinterpreted the nature of these strikes in so far as they were viewed exclusively as 'protests' against the official union bureaucracy. In other words, they did not see that the short sharp strike of the 1950s and 60s was an effective strategy for pursuing material goals in a changed economic and technical situation. In fact, their efforts to use Britain as an illustration of their general thesis led to almost absurdly illogical conclusions.

In the United Kingdom the duration of stoppages has been so brief that we are justified in saying that strikes have been largely eliminated in that country. ([16] p. 19)

In short, our problem will be to explain why strike activity in Great Britain has not 'withered' in all its forms, as it has done in Sweden and the other north European societies of Denmark and Norway, in terms of differences in the levels of institutionalisation of industrial relations to be found between these countries. The theoretical approach to be used in explaining the variations in the levels of institutionalisation is outlined in the following chapter.

3. INSTITUTIONALISATION AND INDUSTRIAL INFRASTRUCTURE

WE have already registered strong agreement with the basic thesis that the development of procedural norms for the regulation of industrial relations is associated with a reduction of strike activity. Quite simply, such norms become an alternative means of resolving conflict. However, strike activity is not related exclusively to the level of institutionalisation of industrial conflict. For example, economists have met with a degree of success in relating economic 'factors' to variations in workers' material demands and positions of power and, in turn, to variations in strike rates. Such studies have focused on both the 'macro' and 'micro' levels. On the one hand, it has been argued that fluctuations in the economy such as the business cycle are among the major determinants of strike activity. Depression and high levels of unemployment are said to weaken labour's bargaining power and consequent inclination and ability to strike. Conversely, prosperity and full employment are said to enhance the workers' power to an extent that they strike quite readily.[1] At best, this kind of approach offers only a partial explanation of the problem : as other writers have pointed out, not all measures of strike rates are equally well correlated with fluctuations in the economy. Evidence from Chapter 2 supports this view. In those countries where the depressions of the 1920s and 30s were most acute – Great Britain, the United States and France – high levels of unemploy-

[1] See, for example, Albert Rees, 'Industrial Conflict and Business Fluctuations', in *Industrial Conflict*, ed. A. Kornhauser *et al.* (New York, 1954); T. Levitt, 'Prosperity versus Strikes', *Industrial and Labor Relations Review*, vi (1952–3).

ment were associated with low strike frequency; but these periods were also characterised by the existence of relatively numerous large-scale, protracted disputes in which a large number of man days were lost. On the other hand, the outbreak of a large number of relatively short strikes, which is often termed an 'explosion' of strike action, is sometimes explained by reference to what may be described as the workers' experience of relative economic deprivation.[2] For example, a recent book has sought to account for the sharp rise in the British strike rate during the 1960s in terms of a fall in workers' real incomes due to inflation and the peculiarities of the British tax structure.[3] Such studies are undoubtedly important, but the implicit theory which lies behind analyses of this kind is of an extremely behaviouristic nature and as such has quite serious limitations. In the first place, relative deprivation may result in discontent and dissatisfaction, but unless the institutional and normative structures of the system are taken into account it becomes difficult to explain the specific form of *action* to which the discontent may lead. To take an obvious and extreme example: in those societies where the strike is made illegal, discontent may take the form of working-to-rule, labour turnover or industrial sabotage, etc. Second, and more fundamentally, expressions of discontent based on feelings of relative deprivation do not occur as direct and automatic responses to changes in objective economic conditions. Deprivation is perceived with reference to some normative standard; but the relationship between norms and expectations is a dialectical one. Norms may serve to inhibit material expectations, but it must be stressed that they do not have unlimited powers of constraint. Drastic changes in an individual's or group's material rewards

[2] Such attempts at explanation are identical to those often found in the study of revolution, though in the former type of study by economists the term 'relative deprivation' is not used. See J. C. Davies, 'Towards a Theory of Revolution', *American Sociological Review* (1962).

[3] Dudley Jackson, H. A. Turner and Frank Wilkinson, *Do Trade Unions Cause Inflation?* (London, 1972). See also Andrew Glyn and Bob Sutcliffe, *British Capitalism, Workers and the Profits Squeeze* (Harmondsworth: Penguin Books, 1972).

may be sufficient to cause them to abandon their compliance with the current legitimation of economic inequality in society. In other words, the institutionalisation of industrial conflict in the form of the emergence of procedural and, especially, substantive norms mediates between objective economic conditions and expressions of discontent, but is itself vulnerable when rapid changes occur in material conditions. Thus, I would argue that the very close and direct relationship between strikes and economic expectations which has been found in Great Britain holds precisely because of the parameter provided by a low level of institutionalisation. That is to say, in recent years the relationship between economic discontent and its expression in strike action has been, in the absence of appropriate regulation, a relatively direct one.

Since the Royal Commission on Industrial Relations it has become commonplace for commentators and social scientists to diagnose Britain's 'strike problem' as one of the relative underdevelopment or inadequacy of existing regulatory institutions. In other words, there is a degree of agreement with Ross and Hartman's theoretical position, if not with their empirical analysis of the British case. However, no adequate explanation of the origins and persistence of this state of affairs has yet been provided. Typically writers have done little more than point out that the structure of British institutions is consistent with certain normative principles which can be identified within these institutions and which, it is argued, have guided their development. Thus, Flanders has on several occasions analysed Britain's complex and decentralised system of industrial relations in terms of its principle of 'voluntarism'.[4] In addition to the empirical problem posed by the fact that a Conservative Government (1970–) whose official ideology espouses such a general principle has been able to abandon it with relative impugnity, such arguments are somewhat circular. No systematic attempt has been made to answer what are, I believe, the fundamentally important questions; that is, if a principle of 'voluntarism' can be discerned within the British system, how did it originate and why has it persisted?

[4] A Flanders, *Industrial Relations: What is Wrong with the System?* (London, 1965).

Moreover, I will suggest in Chapter 5 that, if one looks carefully at these two problems with respect to Great Britain, there are good reasons for asserting that the so-called principle of 'voluntarism' is as much a description of a particular decentralised configuration of power relations as it is an empirically existing norm for the regulation of such relations. Thus the theoretical deficiencies in this area are a particular case of those general problems we looked at in Chapter 1; that is to say, with a few notable exceptions, the study of the development of the institutionalisation of industrial conflict has paid little or no attention to the industrial infrastructures of the societies in which such regulation originates.[5] Frequently, the structure of industrial relations is perceived as comprising only the institutional and value structure.[6] In contrast, the present analysis will make use of the well-established classic sociological tradition which holds that emergence of the normative regulation of social relationships can only be adequately understood by reference to the material structures of society in which such regulation develops.

Western capitalist societies obviously share certain genotypical features in common: factory production; a market economy; formally free labour; private property, etc. Such structures, it is argued, if accompanied by the existence of the liberal democratic state, eventually give rise to the development of a system of free collective bargaining between trade unions and employers. However, the overwhelming emphasis on culture and values as sources of variation in systems of collective bargaining appears to have pre-empted a consideration of important phenotypical variations in the industrial infrastructures of capitalist societies. The present book will, therefore, consider the effects of wide variations in three dimensions of industrial infrastructure on the industrial relations systems of Britain and Scandinavia. I will argue that societies may vary in their degrees of (i) industrial concentration, (ii) what may be called complexity of technical and organisational structure, and (iii) product differentiation and specialisation. These dimensions are not exhaustive, but are considered to be

[5] See J. T. Dunlop [3].
[6] Flanders, op. cit.

38

important in the analysis of the industrial relations systems of the societies in question.

Precise and reliable data on these particular variations in economic systems are scarce. The most comprehensive treatment of *industrial concentration* is still that by Bain, but his data are now more than twenty years old.[7] This particular study used a measure of industrial concentration based upon the 'twenty-plant concentration' in thirty industries in eight countries. Bain calculated the percentage of industrial employment accounted for by the twenty largest plants in the thirty selected industries and expressed these as 'relatives' to the United States. A simplified version of these findings is given in Table 5 below.

TABLE 5

	Median plant concentration relatives
United States	100
Japan	109
Italy	122
France	129
Great Britain	131
India	189
Canada	221
Sweden	234

Source: Bain (1966) p. 47.

Moreover, an examination of the range of 'relatives' shows a startling variation; for example, the least concentrated industry in Sweden shows almost the same concentration as the most con-

[7] Joe S. Bain, *International Differences in the Industrial Structure: Eight Nations in the 1950s* (New Haven, 1966). For a rare excursion by sociologists into the area of industrial infrastructures at the societal rather than the organisational level see Jack P. Gibbs and Hartley L. Browning, 'The Division of Labor, Technology and the Organization of Production in Twelve Countries' in William A. Faunce and William H. Form, *Comparative Perspectives on Industrial Society* (Boston, 1969).

centrated in the United States. The greatest level of concentration in Sweden is over seven times higher than in the United States and nearly two and a half times higher than the highest in Great Britain. In terms of the degree of 'seller concentration' – that is, the degree of control of capacity or output in the hands of relatively few firms – on the basis of very poor data Bain estimated that Great Britain and the United States have the lowest and Sweden the highest concentration. A more recent and smaller study gives general support to Bain's relatively old and otherwise unique data. Pryor used a four-firm concentration ratio – that is, the percentage of value of shipment or production accounted for by the top four enterprises in a narrowly defined industry and also expressed the ratios as relatives to the U.S.A.[8] Table 6 is a simplified presentation of Pryor's findings.

TABLE 6 *Four-firm average concentration ratios as a ratio of concentration ratios in the U.S.A.*

France	0·90
Italy	0·97
West Germany	0·98
United States	1·00
Great Britain	1·04
Japan	1·05
Netherlands	1·17
Belgium	1·46
Switzerland	1·49
Yugoslavia	1·50
Canada	1·52
Sweden	1·58

Source: Pryor (1972).

The degree of concentration is shown by Pryor to be inversely related to the size of the country's domestic market. In other words, those societies in which industrialisation was based upon exports because of too small a domestic market have tended to

[8] Frederic L. Pryor, 'An International Comparison of Concentration Ratios', *Review of Economics and Statistics* (1970) 130–40.

develop highly concentrated industries. Sharp competition in the export field has, in these countries, tended to force out the smaller and less-efficient companies which were less able to contend with fluctuations in world markets.

Variations in the *technical and organisational* complexity of industrial infrastructures are produced by a number of inter-related factors. First, the age of the industrial system is of considerable importance. Those countries which were among the earliest to industrialise have subsequently passed through a number of technological and organisational phases, each of which has influenced the following stage and remains to some degree in the present system. Older systems such as those of Britain and France are of great complexity owing to the movement from a highly competitive economy based on small units with a predominantly craft and workshop technology to a more monopolistic situation in which industrial mass production and automation are of greater importance. Although a similar structural development can be discerned in societies which began their industrialisation at a later time – for example, Sweden and the United States, the earlier workshop structure exerted less influence owing to the availability of mass-production technology. Second, complexity is also related to the level of type of mechanisation in industry. Mechanisation is clearly related to the age of the system but not entirely so; other factors such as the availability of adequate labour at certain stages of development are also important.[9] A low level of mechanisation is often associated with a highly developed division of labour in which manufacture is subdivided into a large number of manual operations and consequently tends to produce a highly complex and differentiated system of production.

Truly comparative and quantitative data on the degree of *product specialisation* in an economy are entirely lacking. The tendency of economists to work with highly simplified aggregate data on industrial production and variations in countries' methods of classifying industries means that any assertions re-

[9] See H. J. Habakkuk, *American and British Technology in the Nineteenth Century* (London, 1967).

garding this particular source of infrastructural variation must remain highly speculative. Nevertheless, I would suggest that those societies which were among the first to industrialise and which possess large domestic markets have tended to produce a wider range of goods than smaller countries which successfully industrialised later to a large extent through the export of highly specialised products.

Each of these closely related dimensions sets a framework on the nature of the power relations between the respective organisations of capital and labour which, in turn, determine to a large extent a society's capacity for developing centralised institutions for the regulation of conflict. The remainder of this chapter is devoted to a brief outline of these relationships and the hypotheses which will guide the subsequent analysis of the industrial relations systems of Britain and Scandinavia.

The possibility of employers organising into a centralised and solidary body with a relatively simple structure would seem to be partly a consequence of the levels of industrial concentration and complexity in an industrial infrastructure. Relatively small-scale societies which export a large part of their manufactured goods tend to have a low level of industrial differentiation and high concentration. In other words, the economy is characterised by a small number of oligopolistic and non-competing sectors. The relatively small number of large-scale employers in each sector facilitates collective organisation and the small employers are constrained to join through the economic impossibility of their taking independent action against the unions. The low level of competition within and between the sectors provides the basis for employer solidarity *vis-à-vis* the unions; that is, employers are free to conclude agreements without jeopardising their economic position in relation to competitors. The existence of a dominant, solidary and powerful employers' association in a society has two important consequences for the development of institutionalisation. First, such an organisation tends to produce 'visible' power relations and clear and specific points of conflict. Other things being equal, this in itself favours the growth of formal regulatory institutions. Second, and more importantly, in such circumstances employers are often able to *impose* normative regulation on the capital–labour relationship. Conversely, an infrastructure with a low level of concentration, high level of complexity and low product specialisation inhibits the growth of a centralised and solidary employers' association.

The structure of a labour movement is similarly related to the nature of the industrial infrastructure in which it is implicated. Complexity, as a result of the historical sequence of different technological stages and/or a low level of mechanisation, and low product specialisation, affect trade union structure through its effect on the division of labour. In short, high levels of complexity and product differentiation tend to be associated with a vast range of occupational groups, skill levels, task specialisms and these result in a differentiated and fragmented trade union structure. Such a structure leads to conflicts of interest within the labour movement and consequently reduces its solidarity, cohesion and capacity for centralisation. The effects of this are similar to those that we noted in the employers' case; that is, a structurally complex and fragmented trade union movement – especially when accompanied by a parallel structure of employers' associations – inhibits institutionalisation. Lines of conflict and power relationships are insufficiently clear and 'visible' to the parties in question to form a basis for purposive and voluntary normative regulation. Conversely, a homogeneous and simple trade union structure permits centralisation and favours institutionalisation.

Moreover, in general terms the mere presence of a complex and differentiated infrastructure reduces the possibility that industry-wide, not to mention national, systems of procedural and substantive normative regulation will be the outcome of industrial class conflict. A fragmented infrastructure makes for a weak and fragmented normative structure unless the latter is imposed and supported by authoritarian political measures.

To sum up, I will argue in the following chapters that high levels of concentration, relatively simple technical and business structures and high levels of product specialisation in the small-scale Scandinavian countries supported the growth of highly centralised employers' associations and labour movements, which, after a period of intense and widespread conflict, resulted in their

43

highly regulated systems of industrial relations. On the other hand, the fragmented bargaining structure and low level of normative regulation in Britain will be placed in the context of the low levels of industrial concentration, product specialisation and infrastructural complexity which shaped its distinctive character.

4. THE DEVELOPMENT OF INDUSTRIAL RELATIONS IN SCANDINAVIA

Sweden: economic development and industrial structure

Swedish economic development accelerated during three short and discontinuous periods : during the 1850s, 1870s and 1890s. However, it is during the latter period and the early twentieth century that the significant changes in Sweden's industrial structure first appeared.[1] Indeed, in comparison with Great Britain, Swedish development was both late and very rapid. In 1870 72 per cent of the Swedish population were engaged in agriculture, forestry and fishing and only 15 per cent in mining, manufacturing and handicrafts; whereas in Great Britain the agricultural population was under 40 per cent as early as 1811 and had further declined to about 10 per cent by the end of the nineteenth century.

Sweden's growth rate in the four decades before the First World War was very rapid. Gross national product increased by 250 per cent during this time and a recent writer has concluded that :

> [Sweden] could show one of the swiftest growth rates of any of those countries which at the beginning of the twentieth century could be regarded as industrialized.[2]

---

[1] Lennart Jörberg, *The Industrial Revolution in Scandinavia* (London, 1970); A. Montgomery, *The Rise of Modern Industry in Sweden* (Stockholm, 1939).

[2] Jörberg, op. cit., p. 25.

Sweden is a small country and with a population of only 4·8 million in 1890 it was a high level of foreign and not domestic demand which led to her economic expansion. During the late nineteenth century there was a shift in exports from timber, pulp and iron ore to engineering products – especially turbines, internal-combustion engines and ball-bearings. Consequently, at the turn of the century Sweden possessed a highly specialised and technologically advanced engineering sector of her industry, which was aimed primarily at the export market. So much so, that this sector had a significantly faster growth rate than those aimed at the domestic market and by 1900 it already employed 25 per cent of those engaged in manufacturing industry, a figure which had increased steadily to 44 per cent by 1958 [13] p. 15. This relatively late industrialisation meant that Sweden was able to take advantage of the existing technology of factory production. Indeed, many important innovations of this kind were developed in Sweden itself. Consequently, the craft basis of manufacturing never became predominant and declined rapidly in the late nineteenth century. In other words, Sweden's leading manufacturing sector was marked by a relatively simple and homogeneous 'industrial' structure at an early stage of its development.

Although firm and plant size was and continues to be generally small by international standards, this leading sector in Swedish industry came to be dominated by a small number of major companies in the early twentieth century.[3] This high level of industrial concentration was, of course, basically dictated by Sweden's reliance on exports which, in addition, led employers to produce a relatively small range of products for highly specialised foreign markets.

As in all industrial societies, concentration steadily increased during the twentieth century and received a further impetus from the rapid rise of mergers during the 1960s.[4] As we saw in the last chapter, comparative data indicate that Sweden has today one

[3] Montgomery, op. cit., p. 168.
[4] Bengt Ryder, 'Concentration and Structural Adjustment in Swedish Industry during the Post-War Period', *Skandinaviska Banken Quarterly Review* (1967, 2) and *Svenska Handelsbanken Economic Review* (1966, 2); (1969, 2).

46

of the most highly concentrated industrial and economic structures in the capitalist world. For example, a Swedish Government inquiry published in 1968 showed that in 1964 the fifty largest companies employed 21 per cent of all workers in private industry and that in 1963 the 100 largest accounted for 46 per cent of private industry's total output.[5] Moreover, this highly concentrated sector of Sweden's economy remains to a large extent in private hands. Fifteen familes together with two corporations have majority control in 200 large industrial concerns that employ almost 50 per cent of all employees in private industry. The most economically powerful of these families is the Wallenburgs: they own a major interest in seventy corporations which employ 20 per cent of all workers in private industry.[6] These data indicate that not only is Swedish industry highly concentrated, but also that, in absolute terms, the *number* of companies accounting for this disproportionate share of industrial production is very small indeed. This characteristic of Sweden's economic structure can be further illustrated by pointing to the relatively small number of large plants in Sweden. In the 1960s Sweden had less than 200 plants employing more than 500 workers; whereas Great Britain had about 3000 and the United States over 6000.[7]

Thus, from the early period of industrialisation up to the present time Swedish industry has been characterised by a high level of concentration of such a kind that a very small number of concerns in the export-based engineering industry have been in a very powerful position in terms of their domination of the labour market and their strategic significance for the economy as a whole.

[5] Statens Offentliga Utredningar, No. 7, *Agande och Inflytande in om det Privata Naringslivet* (Stockholm, 1968) p. 15, quoted in Richard Scase, 'Social Policy and Social Justice: Some comments on Recent Developments in England and Sweden', unpublished paper (1971).

[6] Quoted in Richard F. Tomasson, *Sweden: Prototype of Modern Society* (New York, 1970) p. 224.

[7] Sources: U.S. Bureau of the Census, *Statistical Abstract of the United States*, 1970 (Washington, D.C., 1970) table 712; *Annual Abstract of Statistics, 1969* (London, 1970) table 142; *Nordic Yearbook of Statistics* (1970).

Second, this infrastructure developed initially on the basis of modern industrial factory production and consequently has escaped the complexities of an earlier and influential stage of craft production. Third, it is likely that the crucial significance of exports for the Swedish economy has led to a high level of product specialisation and therefore a relatively undifferentiated industrial structure.

The following section comprises an attempt to relate these features of Sweden's infrastructure to (a) the development, and (b) the present structure, of the system of industrial relations. However, what follows must be seen as a brief and tentative 'sketch'; much more evidence is needed before a more systematic and precise analysis of the problem can be made.

(a) *The development of industrial relations, institutions* The modern Swedish system of industrial relations can be said to have three basic characteristics. First, the employers' associations and the trade unions are highly centralised : the Swedish Confederation of Trade Unions (L.O.) and the Swedish Employers' Confederation (S.A.F.) both exercise almost complete formal and effective power over their respective members. Second, Swedish trade unionism has a very homogeneous structure in so far as manual workers are organised along industrial rather than craft lines.[8] Third, the system is characterised by a high level of formal regulation through industry and nation-wide agreements – that is to say, there is an explicit normative framework on both the *procedural* and *substantive* levels.[9] At the risk of simplifying what

[8] *Craft* unions may be defined as those organisations which organise workers with a particular skill regardless of the place or industry in which they work. *Industrial* unions organise workers in a particular industry regardless of the job they perform. *General* unions are those which organise workers regardless of skill or industry. Eric Hobsbawn has pointed out that general unions may be subdivided into three types. See 'General Labour Unions' in *Labouring Men* (London, 1964).

[9] *Procedural norms* refer to the rules and customs by which employer–worker relationships are regulated. *Substantive norms* refer to the outcome of such regulated relationships – i.e. rates of pay; the length

was a complex process of social development it can be said that the foundations for the structural features of centralisation and industrial unionism were laid in the first decade of the twentieth century. The highly formal and comprehensive normative regulation of the system began to emerge in a clear form later in the 1930s when the central union organisation (L.O.) had finally begun to assume a greater degree of control over its member unions.

The first trade unions were formed during the 1870s and were the craft workers' defensive responses to the abolition of the guilds (1846) and the Economic Freedom Ordinance (1864), which had the effect of removing the inhibitions to capitalist economic development. However, the major impetus to unionisation occurred during the rapid industrialisation of the 1890s. This latter phase of development saw the formation of national and industrial unions based on the emergence of factory production in Sweden's engineering and metal-working industry. The small scale of industrial operations threw up relatively small and financially weak unions which were almost incapable of independent strike action and, therefore, the need for national co-ordination of labour's interests was quickly realised. In 1898 the Confederation of Swedish Trade Unions was formed (Landsorganisajoren i Sverige or L.O.). The L.O. comprised the various national unions and had three main organisational levels – congress, representative assembly and an executive board of five persons (the secretariat). However, its initial authority and functions were fairly limited : strikes and lock-outs were to be reported to the executive board, but the L.O. action was limited to support for strikes in which the employers had taken aggressive action such as cutting wages or locking out newly organised workers. This limitation on the L.O.'s power came from the national unions themselves, who wished to retain their independent powers. At this stage, and for several years to come, the conflict and bargaining in Swedish industry took place between

---

of the working week or day; the way in which work operations are to be carried out, etc. See H. A. Clegg [1] p. 1, and Alan Fox [5] p. 146.

the individual unions and the employers. Indeed, it can be argued that the later development of Sweden's highly centralised and formally regulated system of industrial relations was primarily a consequence of the employers' and not the L.O.'s actions. The economic importance of the engineering and metal-working industry, the high level of concentration and small number of employers provided the structural basis for an Employers' Confederation (S.A.F.), which, in Johnston's words :

Offers a picture of a highly centralised and co-ordinated body which quickly grasped what its objectives were. ([13] p. 68)

Few examples of employers' associations had existed before the 1890s. The traditional employers in iron-ore mining and lumber in central and northern Sweden had, it would seem, little need for such institutions. Rather they exercised a firm paternalistic control – based ultimately on their monopolistic position as buyers of labour – over isolated communities. However, the engineering employers of southern Sweden had to face 'new' groups of industrial workers in a rapidly expanding labour market over which they had more limited economic and social control. From 1882 Stockholm's engineering employers began to organise and in 1896 in Gothenburg a mechanical engineering association was set up to deal with wage claims by the Foundry Workers' Union. Gradually these local associations developed a national unity which took a clearly institutional form in 1902 in response to the workers' political demonstration in support of the franchise. The degree to which industrial concentration and the dominance of a small group of employers provided a viable structural basis for a highly centralised employers' association can be illustrated by the fact that about forty employers met in Stockholm in 1902 and drew up the S.A.F. constitution which has remained virtually unchanged in seventy years ([13] p. 70). The subsequent rapid growth of S.A.F. membership can be understood by reference to the fact that, apart from the few large and dominant companies, Sweden's firms were generally very small and their owners far too weak to tackle the unions without support. Thus, centralisation and solidarity among both unions and employers were

50

in part dictated by the structure and size of the conflicting groups in the Swedish economy.

This rapid centralisation of the S.A.F. allowed employers' leaders to arrive at agreements which were binding on all their members and this clearly affected the individual unions when they negotiated with the S.A.F. For example, the strategically important engineering employers favoured industrial unionism and insisted on national agreements and payment by skill rather than by craft and trade. The eight metal workers' unions were to some extent differentiated on a craft-like basis in terms of the type of metal worked upon and employers were irritated by the cumbersome bargaining process caused by multi-unionism and by minor jurisdictional disputes between crafts.[10] By 1908 the solidarity of the S.A.F. and the widespread and frequent use of the lock-out had proved sufficient to persuade all eight unions to abandon their commitment to an already weakening craft-based organisation and to sign a national agreement. In their Report of that year the S.A.F. were pleased to state that :

It has been shown that the organisations of the workers have not become strong enough to be able to take up a conflict with the existing employers' associations, at least when economic conditions are not overwhelmingly favourable to the workers. ([13] p. 32)

The serious defeat suffered by the labour movement in the General Strike of 1909 broke the resistance of many unions on the craft issue and, although industrial unionism was accepted in principle by the L.O., those craft unions which continued to exist resisted the various plans for the reorganisation of the labour movement.[11] For example, the plan of 1912 to reduce the number

[10] It must be pointed out that the craft principle, although present, was much weaker than in Great Britain for the reason I have already indicated – late industrialisation.

[11] The intense conflict of this period was to a very large extent instigated by the solidary and purposively aggressive S.A.F.: 'Offensively, S.A.F. used the lock-out in the early days to try to adjust the wage level to the state of industry, obtain uniform

51

of unions, by amalgamation, to twenty-one was successfully opposed by the building workers, foundry workers and printers.

Other similar plans were put forward in 1926 and 1951 but achieved little more. In fact the reorganisation plans themselves generally had little direct effect on trade union structure. Rather, owing to bargaining with the solidary and centralised S.A.F., and the increasing concentration of large-scale industry, the craft societies merged with existing industrial unions or combined to form a new union. By 1951 only 10 per cent of L.O. members were in craft unions.

The centralisation of the trade union movement by means of the growth of L.O. power over the member unions was an even more gradual process than the movement from craft to industrial unionism. During the 1909 General Strike the L.O. had exercised powers of control and co-ordination which it did not formally possess, but despite the union defeat many members were reluctant to hand over their powers to the central federation and only minor constitutional changes were made.

The twenty-five years which followed the General Strike of 1909 were marked by intense class conflict which, as we saw in Chapter 2, resulted in a very high level of strike activity and in which individual unions doggedly and generally unsuccessfully confronted the powerful, centralised employers' association (S.A.F.). Several abortive attempts were consequently made during the late 1920s to increase the L.O.'s powers and initiate top-level discussions between the unions and employers, but it was not until the Social Democrats formed a minority government in 1932 that significant changes began to take place in the system of industrial relations. The year 1934 saw a ten-month-long dispute in the building industry in which the unions were weakened financially and the employers threatened a large-scale lock-out.

---

agreements, and develop a settled procedure for negotiations, whereas L.O. had to overcome the parochial and democratic ideals of the national unions. In 1908 and 1909 S.A.F., by contrast to L.O., was able to roll a series of small disputes into the gigantic clash of the Great Strike of 1909, which left L.O. very feeble.' ([13] p. 77.)

The new government's public works policy, which was intended to deal with the economic depression, was disrupted and, fearing government intervention and a possible crushing defeat by the employers, L.O. intervened and brought the strike to a close. The strike was followed by the government-sponsored Nothin Commission, which urged that the L.O. and the S.A.F. rationalise and codify their relationships and hinted that legislation might be required to bring this about. For obvious reasons the powerful and aggressive S.A.F. were against government – especially Social Democratic – intervention in the labour market and the L.O. was anxious to retain its new-found influence. Consequently, in 1936, the two associations began discussions which led to the Basic Agreement of 1938 in which the procedural norms for dealing with disputes were established. It has also been suggested that the L.O. and the S.A.F. were pushed towards negotiations by the equalisation of power which was emerging in the 1930s. The S.A.F. had powers to effect a national lock-out and the LO.'s ability to call a general strike was growing. In other words, the increasing monopolisation of power on each side meant that local conflicts quickly escalated and, it is argued, both parties were in awe of such possibilities. Whatever the particular events and circumstances which immediately led up to the 1938 Basic Agreement, it is crucially important to stress that such an agreement was made possible and could only be sustained by the already existing centralised institutions and their relatively simple and 'visible' power relationship which had been shaped by Sweden's industrial infrastructure. First, the small scale of operations favoured confederation and ultimately centralisation on both sides of industry as most unions and employers were too weak to act independently. Second, the high level of concentration supported the formation of a powerful and solidary employers' association which was prepared to attempt to impose normative regulation in industry. Third, centralisation of the labour movement can be seen as a response to the unions' interaction with the unified employers and which was greatly facilitated by the uniformly modern and simple technical structure of industry which 'late' industrialisation had created in Sweden.

The existence of the Basic Agreement greatly accelerated the growth of the L.O.'s power over its member unions. A revised constitution was accepted in the early 1940s and the L.O.'s *de facto* power duly legitimated. This revision gave the L.O. secretariat almost absolute power over the labour movement.[12] Since this formal centralisation of the L.O.'s powers no radical changes have occurred in the structure of Swedish industrial relations.[13] The L.O. now has the small number of twenty-seven unions whose members comprise over 80 per cent of the male labour force. By the yardstick of international comparison, this figure is extremely high. Below the central level of organisation there are the union branches and the factory 'clubs'. The branch is geographically based and is the level through which the national union carries out its activities and since 1960 their amalgamation has further simplified and centralised trade union structure ([11]). The factory 'club' is a branch subsidiary which provides plant or workshop organisation where the branch covers two or more firms. As in Great Britain, the factory level and not the branch is more important in local bargaining. However, here the similarity ends : the Swedish factory 'club' is firmly controlled by the national union despite the existence of the conflict be-

[12] The L.O. Secretariat gained, among other things, the power to settle inter-union disputes, to draw up policy and to grant or refuse permission for strike action by one or more of the member trade unions. See [13] p. 41.

[13] The most significant developments in Swedish industrial relations since the Second World War have been: (i) The growth of white-collar unionisation. See Arne H. Nilstein, 'White Collar Unionisation in Sweden' in *White-Collar Trade Unions*, ed. A. Sturmthal (London, 1966). (ii) The growth of public employment and new negotiating bodies covering these workers. See also [11] and [7] for analyses of the conflicts these changes have led to. (iii) Accelerated centralisation of the Swedish trade union structure which is clearly associated with the rapid rate of industrial mergers over the last ten years in Sweden. Between 1962 to 1972 the number of trade unions fell from forty-four to twenty-seven mainly through amalgamation ([11]). Lack of space precludes a detailed discussion of these developments; but I would argue that they do not alter my basic thesis concerning industrial infrastructure, the institutionalisation of industrial relations and strikes.

tween rank and file and the leadership which exists to some extent in all large-scale bureaucratised organisations. The close formal relationship between the L.O. and the S.A.F. means that Swedish employees would be unlikely to recognise and negotiate with the kind of shop-steward movement which has grown up in Great Britain. Perhaps the most significant feature of local-level bargaining in Sweden is the absence of multi- or parallel unionism at plant level. Consequently, the normative regulation of industrial relations is made easier than in those societies where craft, religious or political division characterise the labour movement.

We have already looked at the early development of the S.A.F. and its crucial role in the development of Swedish collective bargaining. Its present structure reflects very clearly the increasingly high levels of industrial concentration in Sweden. In 1960 the S.A.F. had forty-four member–employer associations, which accounted for about 66 per cent of the labour force, and, as with the L.O., this figure is extremely high in terms of international comparison. Concentration within the association is also quite marked : over 50 per cent of the employees in all S.A.F. firms are accounted for by only four member associations – the Metal Trades Employers' Association, the General Group, the Building Trades Employers' Federation and the Iron and Steel Association. At firm level the concentration is even more apparent : only 0·8 per cent of S.A.F.'s Partners (the term for individual firms) had more than 1000 employees. but they accounted for 38·8 per cent of all manual employees in S.A.F. At the other end of the scale, 65 per cent of the member firms employed fewer than fifty workers and accounted for only 18 per cent of the manual labour force covered by S.A.F. firms. It is perhaps not surprising that the S.A.F. constitution ensures the dominance of the few large and economically powerful associations and firms in its internal government. Individual employers' associations are required to have over 15,000 employees before they become entitled to appoint a member of the most powerful branch of S.A.F. government – the twenty-eight-man Board. By 1960 this regulation excluded twenty-six of S.A.F.'s forty-four associations from effective participation and influence. There is even a provision for further concentration within the S.A.F. Board, as it has power to appoint an executive committee of two to four members plus the managing director. Direct action is controlled rigidly by the S.A.F. Board; no member association or individual may, in anticipation of a strike, act without S.A.F. permission. Penalties for such independent action are quite severe and range from fines to expulsion from the confederation.

(b) *The present system of regulation*   Since the Basic Agreement of 1938, by which the L.O. and the S.A.F. laid down the procedural norms for the conduct of collective bargaining, there has been a steady growth of national agreements dealing with substantive issues. By 1960 there were 334 such agreements covering 64 per cent of L.O. members; moreover, many so-called local agreements are almost entirely dependent for their content on the national agreements in the various industries. Agreements are extensive and detailed and in addition to wages such issues as accident prevention, work study and job evaluation are dealt with. In fact the range of bargaining issues is much broader than in Great Britain.[14] Since 1956 wage bargaining has taken place, to a large extent, within the framework laid down in centrally negotiated L.O. and S.A.F. agreements. In this way the L.O. and S.A.F. recommend to their members what are considered to be the desirable increases in average hourly earnings for the following two years. There is a degree of flexibility in the system in so far as the actual implementation of the recommendations is effected through union-level bargaining. However, the degree of control the L.O. and the S.A.F. exercise over their members prevents most open opposition to or disregard of the central agreement. Plant bargaining is further restricted as strikes and other industrial action are prohibited by law during the period an agreement is in force.

Thus, I would wish to argue that the particular form the institutionalisation of industrial relations has taken in Sweden inhibits strike activity for three interrelated reasons. First, the Swedish industrial infrastructure and its centralised institutions

[14] Lester [15] p. 399.

56

produce a relative equality of organisational power between capital and labour and this, through fear of escalation, reduces strike activity.[15] Second, the 'visibility' of each side's power and intentions means that strikes are not frequently used as a bargaining strategy or as a means of discovering and testing their strengths and weaknesses. Third, the centralised institutions and the nature of their power relationship has favoured the development of a very formal and comprehensive system of normative regulation which inhibits strike action by providing alternative means for the settlement of disputes. This does not, of course, mean that class conflict as such has been eradicated in Sweden, but given the extreme nature of the normative and factual constraints on striking it is expressed in other forms such as 'go-slows' and possibly high levels of labour turnover.[16]

Obviously strikes do continue to occur in Sweden and when they do break out the centralised system and 'visible' power relationships often produce large-scale protracted disputes in which the sides frequently reach entrenched positions. Moreover, as we have noted, the incidence of strike activity in Sweden is much higher than the official statistics record. Fulcher, who has brought these data to the attention of English sociologists, argues that:

in the Swedish case, more and more open conflict appears as one descends from the central level of organisational interaction to the shop floor. The pattern of this conflict and its similarity with that of other industrial societies suggests that whatever the superstructure, the economic and technological substructure impose their own pattern. ([7] p. 54)

Fulcher's argument is that in Sweden, like other advanced capitalist societies, full employment and the increasing capital intensiveness and structural interdependence of modern industry bring power to workers at the shop-floor level. This change from

[15] For an elaboration of this argument see R. Dubin, 'A Theory of Conflict and Power in Union–Management Relations', *Industrial and Labor Relations Review* (1960) p. 501.

[16] H. A. Turner *et al.*, *Labour Relations in the Motor Industry* (London, 1967) p. 321.

the nineteenth century, when workers' power depended on their level of unionisation, produces a high strike rate in modern industries such as metal-working, engineering and especially the motor-car industry. Pressure on wages from certain sections of the labour force in a situation of full employment results in what has become known as the 'wage-drift' – that is, earnings rise in excess of negotiated wage rates. Increases which come about in this way are, of course, disruptive of established differentials within the labour force of any society, but especially so in Sweden because of their effects on the L.O.'s 'wages solidarity' policy. Since the Second World War the L.O. have attempted to narrow wage differentials by awarding disproportionate increases to lower-paid workers and, clearly, the local bargaining of those workers favoured by the labour market situation could potentially undermine these efforts. Consequently, as Fulcher suggests, a conflict between powerful groups of rank-and-file workers and the central trade union leadership may be emerging in Sweden. In addition, Fulcher points out that the well-organised 'middle-class' unions are anxious to preserve income differentials in the face of what they perceive as working-class affluence and are consequently in conflict with both employers and the manual workers ([7]). All this, it is argued, has led to a breakdown of the industrial stability of the 1950s and early 1960s which is evidenced in the increasing difficulties experienced in central wage negotiations since 1966 ([7] and [11]). The 1970 official strike figures add some substance to these assertions: 128 strikes were recorded, which is three times higher than the next-highest figure of forty-five in 1954.

Fulcher is, of course, right to counter the often-inaccurate eulogies of the Swedish system, but in his effort to stress the similarities exhibited by all advanced capitalist societies he appears to have overstated his case. In the first place, recent economic research has suggested that the nature of inflation and the 'wage-drift' in Sweden are such that their consequences are less disruptive than in other societies. It has been argued by Swedish economists that the existence in the Swedish economy of a distinct and internationally competitive sector can, because of an annual 1 per cent increase in world prices, absorb the wage demands

58

of the sheltered domestic sector.[17] It may be noted in passing that this analysis of the Swedish economy supports the present characterisation of the sectoral nature of Sweden's infrastructure. Second, conflict may indeed be increasing in Sweden; but it is difficult to demonstrate that this is manifested in an increasing strike rate. The number of officially recorded strikes did rise sharply to 128 in 1970. However, this cannot be taken to indicate a trend : the number of strikes for the years 1966–9 were 26, 7, 7 and 32. Obviously there are problems with the official statistics but all evidence indicates that the Swedish strike rate is extremely low and this is in striking contrast with many other advanced industrial countries. Despite the structural changes and possible increase in 'latent' conflict the Swedish system continues to show a remarkable facility for inhibiting and constraining strike action. Finally, Fulcher's argument is based on his view that industrial societies have a similar 'economic and technological substructure'. This is only partially correct. It is, by definition, the case that advanced industrial societies have infrastructural features in common, but, as I have stressed, some of these features can vary to such a degree that they are involved in the development of significantly different institutional and normative arrangements. Fulcher sees the emergence of a contradiction between 'substructure' and 'institutional superstructure' in Sweden's industrial relations system, whereas I would contend that the absence of such a contradiction has been and continues to be a basic feature of Swedish society. I do not, of course, mean that there is no contradiction, in the classic Marxian sense, between capital and labour, nor that there are no new sources of conflict and tension in Swedish society; but in the absence of extreme economic dislocation Sweden's institutional structure will contain conflict to a degree unlikely to occur in, say, Great Britain.[18]

In concentrating on the implications of Sweden's industrial

[17] G. Edgren, K. O. Faxen and C. E. Odhner, 'Wages, Growth and the Distribution of Income', *Swedish Journal of Economics* (September 1969).

[18] After the difficulties that arose in the 1970–1 negotiations the L.O. and the S.A.F. have already (1972) embarked upon direct discussions and collaboration in an attempt to forestall problems

infrastructure for her system of industrial relations I would hope that I have not implied a crude deterministic explanation. In the first place, industrial infrastructures must be viewed as setting constraints on possible courses of action. Within this framework many varied developments could have taken place. Even a cursory glance at the history of Swedish industrial relations shows the importance of key historical events. For example, the process toward industrial unionism was accelerated by the severe defeat suffered by the unions in the 1909 General Strike; but it cannot be asserted that the employers' victory was, in any way, inevitable. Furthermore, Sweden's neutrality in the First World War allowed her to escape the worst of the post-war depressions which weakened and demoralised many European labour movements including that in Great Britain. Thus, when the opportunity arose in the 1930s, Sweden's L.O. was able to negotiate with the S.A.F. on more or less equal terms and backed by a steadily growing membership. Had Sweden experienced the social and economic disorganisation the war created, it is beyond question that, the structure of industry notwithstanding, the development of the industrial relations system would have been different. Second, it would be naïve to imply that factors other than those I have stressed were not involved in this process of development. The glaring omission, which this brief treatment made necessary, has been the neglect of the possible independent role of the state and political structures in general.[19]

---

which may occur in the 1973 negotiations. Thus, the trend in Sweden is to *continuous* planning and co-ordination in industrial relations. In other words, there is an attempt to define, *in advance*, the problems which may be encountered [11].

[19] Many other commentaries place emphasis on the Swedes' commitment to 'rationality' or other such values as an explanation of the Swedish system. A typical example is that offered by Charles A. Myers, 'Management in Sweden', *Management in the Industrial World*, ed. Frederick Harbison and Charles A. Myers (New York, 1959): '. . . there is fairly general agreement with a British writer [Arthur Spencer, *The Economist* (1954)] that Sweden's "law-abiding tradition" and "abhorence of extremes" . . . combine to curb

Norway and Denmark

The other Scandinavian countries in the present study where strike activity has declined dramatically since the Second World War – namely Norway and Denmark – share two other important characteristics with Sweden. First, their processes of industrial development which accelerated rapidly in the late nineteenth century were in varying degrees export-based and this factor together with the small scale of the societies has led to a high level of industrial concentration. Second, both countries developed centralised institutions for collective bargaining which have been associated with highly formal and comprehensive norms for the regulation of industrial relations. There are, of course, some important differences between the societies, some of which – such as the well-developed craft unionism in Denmark – might be thought to be inimical to the growth of the kind of institutions and regulatory norms which, I have argued, inhibit strike activity. However, we shall see that certain infrastructural similarities appear to limit the degree to which such variations have been able to exert an independent influence on the systems of collective bargaining in question.

Norway Of the two societies we are looking at, Norway is most similar to Sweden in all important respects. Like its northern European neighbours, it is a small society: in 1969 the non-agricultural labour force was only about 1·2 million. Consequently, industrialisation had to await the growth of world demand for Norwegian exports in the late nineteenth century.[20] Shortly after the 1850s timber and engineering were the major exporting industries; but with the introduction of hydro-electric power in the 1890s electro-chemical and electro-metallurgical factories began to assume great importance. For example, by 1909 Norway produced 20 per cent of the world's production of calcium carbide. Thus, by the beginning of the twentieth century

---

excesses by either side of industry' (p. 299). The general difficulties associated with this type of reasoning were noted in Chapter 1.

[20] Jörberg, op. cit., p. 64.

Norwegian industry was dominated by a small number of economically powerful companies in the strategic export-based industries. There is little direct evidence on levels of industrial concentration for either the early period or the present day; but the scale of operation in Norwegian industry was clearly very small. In 1968 there were only 276 establishments, each with over 200 workers, but they accounted for about 30 per cent of all employees in private industry. Moreover, as we noted in Chapter 3, there are sound theoretical reasons for concluding that small industrial societies with limited domestic markets are likely to have very high levels of industrial concentration.

This particular form of industrial infrastructure has, as in Sweden, formed the basis for the growth of highly centralised workers' and employers' organisations ([8] [10]). Indeed, the level of centralisation appears to be even higher than in Sweden and this was probably made possible by the extremely small scale of industrial operations. In other words, neither individual unions nor employer's associations have been, at any stage, large enough to secure a financial base for independent action: the founding of the Norwegian Federation of Labour (A.F.L.) with its central strike fund in 1899 enabled the unions to engage successfully in industrial action and survive the employers' lockouts ([10] p. 131). The central power of the Federation was extended in 1945 and at the present time wage policy is almost completely determined by the Federation in close collaboration with the Labour Government, which leaves the individual unions in an almost powerless position. The Norwegian Employers' Association was formed in 1900 and – as in Sweden – the Association has, throughout its history, favoured a highly centralised and hierarchical form of organisation with permanent full-time officials and a chief executive.

Industrial unionism became the major principle of organisation in the early twentieth century and was brought about by the growth of new factory-based industries and the desire of the employers for industry-wide bargaining. The weakly established craft groups were unable to resist this development and often merged to form a new industrial union. By the 1940s 85 per cent of the A.F.L.'s members were in fifteen industrial unions and the remaining 15 per cent in craft organisations.

The course of events leading up to the regulation of industrial relations by means of agreements between the Employers' Association and the Federation of Labour is, once again, remarkably similar to that which occurred in Sweden. By the 1920s the two organisations began to exercise their powers by calling large-scale strikes and lock-outs. However, the equality of the power relationship between the two parties provided only a few decisive conclusions to disputes and in 1935 they drew up a Basic Agreement. This agreement laid down the basic procedural norms for the regulation of collective bargaining in Norway, which usually results in multi-employer, industry-wide contracts.

Thus I would argue that since the 1930s the reduction of uncertainty in collective bargaining by means of highly specific and formal normative regulation based upon relatively homogeneous and solidary organisations and a visible power structure in industry has inhibited strike activity.

Denmark The development and structure of industrial relations in Denmark differ in some respects from what we have seen to be the case in Sweden and Norway, but the similarities of both the industrial infrastructure and basic system of industrial relations are clearly apparent.

The very small domestic market in Denmark again meant that the economic expansion which occurred in the 1890s had to be based upon exports. However, in this case the exported products were agricultural rather than industrial: before 1890 there was virtually no exportation of manufactured goods.[21] Nevertheless, this agriculturally based economic growth provided a basis for manufacturing industry. On the one hand Danish agriculture was highly mechanised and there developed a sector of the metal industry which specialised to meet these needs. On the other hand the agriculturally based growth of income eventually stimulated manufacturing industry in general and Denmark began to acquire an international reputation for the production of quality goods for export – for example, silverware, porcelain, marine

[21] Ibid.

engines and beer. As one would expect, this particular course of development produced an industrial infrastructure which differs somewhat from those in Norway and Sweden. Briefly, the economic reliance on agriculture enabled the craft-based industries to persist, and consequently industrial unionism is only a minor part of the Danish system of industrial relations. However, industrial concentration does not appear to be significantly different from the levels to be found in Sweden and Norway. By 1872 there were only thirty-seven firms in Copenhagen employing more than 100 workers and they accounted for over half the capital's labour force and by 1967 Denmark had only ninety enterprises which employed more than 500 workers, but they, in fact, had over 30 per cent of the total labour force in private industry. Moreover, the concentration in Denmark is also geographical in nature. A large proportion of Danish industry is concentrated in and around Copenhagen : by 1935 the capital contained 21·8 per cent of all industrial establishments and 40·4 per cent of the industrial labour force ([9] p. 76).

Despite the craft structure the Danish trade unions federated in 1898 (Danish Federation of Labour – D.S.F.) when the small independent unions became aware of their weaknesses in face of the solidary and aggressive Copenhagen employers. The craft societies, in fact, welcomed this centralisation as they were already secure in their jurisdictions and able to command a majority vote in the annual congress. These unions have co-operated closely throughout their history and recently moved towards a degree of amalgamation ([14] p. 173); but their desire for craft autonomy has meant that of the three Scandinavian labour federations the Danish has the least power. It must, of course, be stressed that by British standards the powers it does possess are quite considerable.

The centralisation that does exist in Danish industrial relations is to a large extent, as in Sweden and Norway, related to the solidarity of the Danish employers. The institution of their federation in 1898 was merely the formal expression of well-established co-operative action against the workers and, like the Swedish S.A.F., they pressed at an early date for national agreements and industrial unionism.

Although they failed in the virtually impossible task of persuading the unions to abandon their craft organisation, the employers' aggression drove the unions to seek protection through close mutual co-operation. The small scale of operations and concentration of industry had given the Danish employers a basis for organisation and solidarity which they clearly used. Between 1898 and 1946 a total of 343,000 workers went on strike; but in the same period over 330,000 were also locked out. During many lock-outs during the early twentieth century unaffiliated employers often attempted to win over the customers of the Association employers involved in the lock-out, and it is a measure of the Association's solidarity that many such 'lock-out breakers' were financially ruined when, after the lock-out, the Association members cut off commercial relations with them ([9] p. 87).

As in Sweden and Norway, industrial relations during the 1920s and early 1930s were characterised by widespread open conflict which was not only supported but frequently initiated by the two central organisations. By the early 1930s, after a series of agreements which introduced procedures for regulating employer-worker relations, a comprehensive and detailed normative framework began to emerge. Thus, since the late 1930s almost continuous regulated negotiation between the powerful central organisations has been associated with very limited strike activity and the almost total disappearance of the lock-out. However, the recent General Strike in Denmark (1973) serves as a reminder that, when they do occur, strikes are likely to be large-scale and often protracted owing to the highly centralised bargaining structure.

5. THE DEVELOPMENT OF INDUSTRIAL RELATIONS IN GREAT BRITAIN

IN all but the most superficial respects the system of industrial relations in Great Britain offers a marked contrast to those of the Scandinavian countries. Great Britain possesses a complex, differentiated and relatively decentralised institutional system which has not led to the formal and comprehensive normative regulation of industrial relations we have found in these other north European countries. To be sure, Great Britain does share some features in common with Scandinavia; but, as I have implied, these similarities are more apparent than real. For example, any comparison of the respective central labour organisations – such as the Swedish L.O. and the British T.U.C. – must not take their mere existence as an indication of overwhelming similarity. These organisations possess immense power in Scandinavia, whereas the T.U.C. has displayed chronic constitutional and *de facto* weakness throughout its entire history.

The particular characteristics of the British system of industrial relations – that is to say, its complexity, differentiation, relative decentralisation and low levels of formal normative regulation – are, I believe, partly explicable in terms of the structure of industry within which they developed. Quite simply, many of the major differences between British and Scandinavian industrial relations are related to variations in the type and timing of their earlier stages of capitalist economic development.

Economic development and industrial infrastructure.
The characteristics of complexity, product differentiation and relatively low industrial concentration have been present in vary-

ing degrees at all stages of Britain's industrial development and the sources of all three features may be traced to two consequences of Britain's role as the first industrial society.

First, manufacturing industry in this country has passed through a number of different technological and organisational phases each of which influenced subsequent stages and all of which remain in some degree in the present industrial infrastructure. Such a process, I will argue, makes for a high level of complexity. There appears to be some agreement that three distinct processes may be identified. Touraine sees them as interpenetrating or overlapping stages of development: the workshop phase; the mechanical or division-of-labour phase and the continous-process or automated phase. Moreover, in a similar manner to the present study, it is argued that the continued coexistence of all three stages may account, in part, for the multifaceted and intense nature of industrial conflict in modern French society.[1] While not analysing the uneven historical development of stages of industrial production, Woodward has also identified three types of technological process: small-batch (mainly craft); mass-production and continous-process.[2]

The earliest phase in British manufacturing industry in the early and mid-nineteenth century was based upon craft technology and the small-scale workshop form of organisation.[3] Even cotton manufacturing, which was more 'industrial' in character than most early British industry, exhibited this kind of structure. Here Hobsbawm refers to an 'extremely decentralised and disintegrated business structure' in which firms or workshops specialised in only one of the many stages of production, such as spinning, weaving, dyeing etc.[4] Moreover, he suggests that such

[1] For an English summary of Touraine's type of analysis see Charles Posner, 'Introduction' to *Reflections on the Revolution in France: 1968* (Harmondsworth: Penguin Books, 1970).

[2] Joan Woodward, *Industrial organisation: Theory and Practice* (London, 1965).

[3] H. J. Habakkuk, *American and British Technology in the Nineteenth Century* (Cambridge, 1962).

[4] E. J. Hobsbawm, *Industry and Empire* (Harmondsworth: Penguin Books, 1969).

a pattern was common to all British industry at this time. Thus, the early primitive technology and the absence of any significant vertical integration of industrial processes meant that, within the emerging industries, employers were fragmented and workers highly differentiated along craft lines. The subsequent development of larger-scale mass-production industry in the late nineteenth and early twentieth centuries was crucially affected by this early stage. Indeed, it became commonplace to explain the decline of Britain's economic dominance at the end of the nineteenth century by pointing to the fact that her chief competitors – Germany and the United States – had developed efficient mass-production industries unfettered by obsolete plant and inappropriate forms of business organisation.[5] Today, it is perhaps only the very modern industries – such as petro-chemicals and electronics – that have largely escaped this particular legacy of the nineteenth century.

The second important consequence of Britain's pioneering role as an industrial society is that up to the last quarter of the nineteenth century she was the world's only large-scale producer of manufactured goods – 'the workshop of the world'. In the absence of serious foreign competition Britain's entrepreneurs produced a vast range of goods for both domestic and foreign markets and in doing so added the characteristics of product diversity and differentiation to the industrial infrastructure. Furthermore, the absence of foreign competition allowed very rapid

[5] See G. C. Allen, *British Industries and their Organization*, 1st edn (London, 1933); A. J. Levine, *Industrial Retardation in Britain 1880–1914* (London, 1967); S. B. Saul, *The Myth of the Great Depression* (London, 1969), for discussions of the issues involved. Something of a heated debate has grown up in economic history regarding the reasons for Britain's 'decline' during this period. For one of the latest ventures in the field see D. C. Coleman, 'Gentlemen and Players', *Economic History Review*, 2nd series, xxvi, 1 (1973) 92–116. Some writers stress strictly economic and technological factors, while others hold that British entrepreneurs were conservative and amateur, and distrusted science and innovation. The debate's relevance to the present problem is obvious, but regrettably cannot be discussed here.

expansion in which manufacturers were not constrained to combine in order to secure economies of scale. To be sure, legislation earlier in the century had made the large monopolistic joint-stock company a possibility, but it would seem that the opportunities it afforded were not taken up seriously until the early twentieth century.[6] Exactly how far the workshop stage of production inhibited later development is difficult to establish with any degree of accuracy, but as some recent commentators have suggested :

> the need to cater for widely differing tastes and specifications made firms reluctant to adopt any policy of standardization or surrender their independence by combining with other producers.[7]

The third persistent characteristic of Britain's economy – namely, the low level of concentration – is, then, the result of both the above interrelated factors. The large diversified markets, the rapid expansion of industry and the predominantly workshop technology resulted in an industrial infrastructure which

> emerged as and largely remained a complex of highly specialised firms of medium size . . . linked to each other by a complex of individual business transactions in the 'market'.[8]

Clearly British industry has changed considerably in the last fifty years. On the one hand, these changes have involved the successive developments of mass-production and automated industries which, from the outset, were marked by large-scale companies and greater levels of concentration than nineteenth-century industry. On the other hand, the old staple industries

[6] P. L. Payne, 'The Emergence of the Large-Scale Company in Great Britain, 1870–1914', *Economic History Review*, 2nd series, xx (1967) 519.

[7] J. H. Dunning and G. J. Thomas, *British Industry: Change and Development in the 20th Century* (London, 1961) p. 39. See also Habakkuk, op. cit., pp. 210–11.

[8] Hobsbawm, op. cit., pp. 64–5.

of the nineteenth century have declined and in the process changed their structure. To continue with our example, there has been a rapid decline in the number of firms in the cotton industry by means of both 'mortality' and merger. Vertical integration, especially of spinning and weaving, has ultimately led to higher levels of concentration, but dispersion is still a major feature of the industry. No adequately detailed data in support of this assertion appear to be available, but in an industry with a similar history and structure – the woollen and worsted industry – employment in the three largest enterprises amounted to no more than 9 per cent of the industry's total in 1958. This offers a marked contrast to the much newer man-made fibre industry in which, in 1958, the three largest firms accounted for 81 per cent of the total employment in that industry.[9] However, despite these changes, we saw in Chapter 3 that two detailed studies placed the modern British economy as one of the least concentrated in the industrial world.[10]

Although there are no data that could be seriously used to demonstrate the case, it must be assumed that the period during the twentieth century during which Britain has faced foreign competition was one in which product diversity and differentiation were reduced. However, it cannot be safely said that our other characteristic – complexity – has diminished in any way. Clearly, there are immense problems in measuring 'complexity'. Nevertheless I would wish to argue that the coexistence of the three technological and organisational phases in present-day industry creates a degree of complexity to at least match that which was present in the earlier transitional stage from workshop technology to mass production.

The following two sections comprise (i) an analysis of the industrial relations institutions in Britain as they develop within the infrastructural framework I have outlined, and (ii) a brief description of the present system of normative regulation and its relationship to Britain's so-called 'strike problem'.

[9] G. C. Allen, *The Structure of Industry in Britain*, 3rd edn (London, 1970) p. 251.
[10] See Chapter 3.

(i) *The development of industrial relations institutions*

As in the Scandinavian case I believe that much light can be shed on the nature of the British system of industrial relations by focusing on the action – or rather in this case the inaction – of her employers. Therefore, I will begin this account somewhat unconventionally by looking at the growth of their organisations and associations.

Associations between employers in the same or related industries or crafts were common in the early and mid-nineteenth century as the 1867 Royal Commission revealed.[11] However, these associations were almost exclusively local and commercial in character. Employers met informally to attempt to fix prices and wages to their mutual advantage; but only sporadically did their organisation extend to presenting a united front to the growing unions. Of course, some employers had little need to combine, as their workers were only weakly organised, and others, when faced with unions, steadfastly refused to recognise their existence. In short, the structure of industrial relations in nineteenth-century Britain was similar to that which can be observed in most societies undergoing industrialisation; that is to say, the level of institutionalisation was low. However, in the British case we shall see that the extension of regulation was both slow and limited and this situation is closely related to the complexity, dispersion and differentiation of the industrial infrastructure. In the later nineteenth century when, after fifty years of industrial activity, institutionalisation of the basic capital–labour relationship began to develop only rarely did it result in highly formal industry-wide agreements. Moreover, even where this did occur – such as in building and cotton – the basic bargaining issues of

[11] The following account is based on Clegg [1] pp. 118–54. There is no general history of employers' associations in Great Britain. Clegg explains this as a consequence of the employers' secretive attitude to their business. But it seems more likely that this neglect stems from the fact that workers and unions have been conceptualised by historians and sociologists as a recalcitrant 'social problem'; whereas employers and their associations belong to the natural order of things and, as such, require no comment.

pay and conditions continued to be dealt with on a firm or district level. British employers, unlike their Scandinavian counterparts, did not press for formal industry-wide regulation. In the Swedish case, especially, we saw that self-consciously organised and cohesive employers are quite capable of imposing regulatory norms on industrial relations during the early stages of industrialisation; but British employers displayed no such solidarity and common aim. Rather, it would seem that the dispersed and differentiated industrial infrastructure, which has sustained a commitment to *laissez-faire*, inhibited such action in Great Britain. In general, British industry at the time contained no group of capitalists who were strong enough, let alone willing, to impose regulation on the system. The small and medium-sized British employers were differentiated by product and process to a degree which, in itself, precluded common goals and, in addition, where common interests did exist, the highly competitive nature of the economy prevented their articulation in a formal manner. In other words, many employers were wary of any detailed and formal regulation which, they argued, might prevent their securing an advantage over competitors in a future situation of changed economic circumstances.

Obviously, the twentieth century has witnessed a move among British employers towards more formal organisation and centralisation. Employers were increasingly unable to ignore the organisational strength of the unions and were constrained by the logic of the situation to set up complementary bodies. These developments were facilitated by the increasing concentration of industry which was closely related to the growth of the large corporation. However, despite such changes, the organisation of British employers was and continues to be far less marked than in Scandinavia, and two reasons may be adduced for this difference. First, as I have already suggested, the infrastructural changes in Britain towards more concentration were not sufficiently large to encourage the growth of solidary associations of employers. What little evidence exists points to the persistence of modes of organisation and orientations to action which are clearly traceable to the earlier period of industrialisation I have outlined. Second, the British state played a far greater role in industrial

73

relations than was the case in any of the Scandinavian countries. On the one hand, this is clearly a consequence of direct government action in British industry that was required during the two World Wars. Sweden did not participate in either war and although Denmark and Norway were occupied during the Second World War this had little direct effect on the structure of collective bargaining after 1945. On the other hand, Britain's role as an imperial power and the general growth of government intervention in domestic affairs during the nineteenth century meant that a relatively strong and active state was available to come to the aid of the capitalist classes when crises have made it necessary.

Before 1914 there were, in fact, several abortive attempts by the employers to organise centrally, but for the reasons I have outlined national co-ordination was successful only during explosions of worker militancy and this temporary solidarity did not lead to any permanent intervention in the labour market.[12] This chronic fragmentation before 1914 is all the more remarkable if one notes that a central, if weak, union organisation (T.U.C.) had existed for nearly fifty years. As I have suggested, the situation changed during the First World War: the war effort required the efficient co-ordination and control of basic industries and services and the government realised that the co-operation of the unions was essential. Consequently, regulation of industrial relations was extended by such means as Joint Industrial Councils in the hope of avoiding damaging disputes. In

[12] Although it is dubious practice to draw on isolated points of comparison, it is worth while noting that, with respect to the United States (with even greater differentiation, lower concentration and internal competition than Great Britain), an early commentator suggested that: 'Associations tend to become strong during later troubles or when there is threatened legislation. . . . Likewise they tend to disintegrate during periods of peace.' (Clarence E. Barrett, *Employers' Associations in the United States* (New York, 1922).) For a discussion of a period (1880s and 1890s) when the British did organise and act aggressively see H. A. Clegg, Alan Fox and A. F. Thompson, *A History of British Trade Unions since 1889* vol. I, *1889–1910* (Oxford, 1964) chapter 4.

some instances the employers were almost completely by-passed; for example, the railway- and ship-owners, who had traditionally been hostile to the unions, were drawn into formal agreements with them under the constraint of state control of their industries. Even in those industries which avoided direct state control, government intervention in labour relations in the form of Courts of Inquiry and Tribunals spurred employers into organisation for a more adequate representation of their interests. The steady growth of industry-based employers' organisations eventually led to national associations – but there was little centralisation of the kind which occurred in Scandinavia. In the first place, *three* organisations were formed : the National Union of Manufacturers (1915); the Federation of British Industries (1917) and the National Confederation of Employers' Organisations (1920). Second, the new institutions clearly manifested their origins as a defensive response to the encroachments on the prerogatives of private capital by the state and the unions. Once formed the three bodies took little initiative in extending the industry and nation-wide collective bargaining procedures the government had encouraged during the war. Common policy was not developed in any purposive and systematic way and it seems that commercial matters rather than industrial relations were the employers' main interest. Indeed, during the early 1920s when government intervention was reduced the employers demonstrated a clear unwillingness to fill the vacuum and

since then [the First World War] important innovations in the industry-wide conduct of industrial relations, when they have occurred, have been inspired by the government. ([1] p. 129)

As a consequence of the complex, dispersed and differentiated infrastructure – and the decentralised institutions it has fostered – only very rarely, in the past, has overt industrial conflict become general throughout British industry. This is quite a different pattern from the large-scale Scandinavian disputes that preceded the comprehensive regulation of industrial relations that took place in the 1930s. Nevertheless, the British experience of a

General Strike did lead to one attempt at the centralised regulation of collective bargaining that became commonplace in Scandinavia. The ultimate fate of this attempt in the shape of the Mond–Turner talks and Report (1927–8) shows in stark relief the different patterns of development of the institutionalisation of industrial conflict in the societies in question. Before the 1920s there had been several almost totally insignificant attempts at central worker–employer collaboration with the aim of avoiding overt industrial conflict; for example, the proposal in 1894 for an Industrial Union of Employers and Employed; the short-lived National Alliance of Employers and Employed (1917) and the 1919 proposals for an Industrial Parliament. The explanation for their failure is simple and obvious: without a nationally unified employers' organisation such proposals could not even progress to the stage where they might have ultimately foundered on the basic economic conflicts of a capitalist society. The discussions in 1927–8 between Sir Alfred Mond (later Lord Melchett), Chairman of the newly formed Imperial Chemical Industries, other leading industrialists and the General Council of the T.U.C. achieved very little more; but, as I have suggested, the events are illustrative of many structural features of the development of British industrial relations. Chastened by the experiences of the General Strike, George Hicks, the President of the T.U.C., made a public statement which amounted to an invitation to British employers to join with the T.U.C. in an attempt to centrally regulate and rationalise the chaotic structure of collective bargaining. The major employers' associations remained silent, but Sir Alfred Mond responded and began talks with Ben Turner of the T.U.C. The proposals of the subsequent Mond–Turner Report were far-reaching; they included a strong plea for greater centralisation and an assertion that an influence on government economic policy fell within the legitimate province of both capital and labour. Despite left-wing union opposition the T.U.C. were prepared to accept the recommendations; but the employers, in the shape of the British Employers' Confederation, to whom the Report was also submitted, displayed wilful intransigence. In G. D. H. Cole's opinion they did not even see the need to offer the unions the very subordinate role in shaping economic policy and industrial relations which Mond was ready to concede.[13] In line with their persistent belief, the individual employers wished to avoid any form of comprehensive regulation for fear that this might either tie their own hands in dealings with their labour force or be exploited by the unions when economic circumstances permitted. As Clegg states :

> The Confederation had clearly indicated to individual employers that the path to reform in industrial relations did not lie through the employers' associations. If they wanted reform they must pursue it in their own companies through their personnel policies. ([1] p. 133)

Thus the unions were willing to collaborate but the employers persisted with their *laissez-faire* orientation. It is, in fact, most significant that it was Mond who took up the initial T.U.C. invitation. First, Mond and his company remained outside the formal employers' organisations and, second, he was the head of a large economically powerful company in a modern industry which was free of the constraints of the nineteenth-century infrastructure. However, Britain was too large and complex and Mond's I.C.I. and his associates too small to permit the imposition of a system of regulation on the society in the way the dominant Swedish employers had done through the medium of their solidary employers' association.

The period up to the 1950s saw some extension of collective bargaining in the form of industry-wide agreements. However, all the available evidence suggests that the employers preferred minimal regulation of pay and conditions and consequently they made little effort to centralise and co-ordinate their associations. The greatest changes in this respect have occurred during the 1960s. On the one hand, the rapid rate of mergers of various kinds encouraged amalgamations of many local employers' associations and ultimately the formation of a single central employers' association (Confederation of British Industry, 1965) almost one hundred years after the founding of the T.U.C.

[13] G. D. H. Cole, *British Trade Unionism* (London, 1939).

77

On the other hand, the growth of detailed regulatory norms in the form of 'productivity agreements' between individual companies and unions has had the effect of drawing the organised British employers into a more active role in industrial relations. Productivity bargains necessarily require a detailed and precise framework for adjusting pay to changes in the organisation of work and workers' performances and they often clash with the existing industry-wide regulation agreements between the unions and the relevant employers' associations. It is significant that the first and most renowned of these 'bargains' – the Fawley Productivity Agreement – was negotiated by the non-federated Esso Company. Indeed the members of the employers' associations were indifferent and at times openly hostile to such innovations in the regulation of industrial relations and some companies such as Alcan left their employers' association in order to be completely free to conclude their own productivity bargain. Such events persuaded the Confederation of British Industry to attempt to integrate this new type of bargaining into the existing system and thus British employers as a body began to take a more positive and active role in shaping the regulation of industrial conflict. Lest it may be thought that these recent changes constitute a dramatic break with past structure and history it is useful to note some of the conclusions reached in the Donovan Report (1968). First, despite amalgamations, it was found there were still about 1350 employers' associations in existence – compared with only forty-four in Sweden (1961). Furthermore the vast majority of the associations are not members of the C.B.I.; but in Scandinavia such independent existence would be unthinkable. Second, it was discovered that, beyond the recently instituted C.B.I., organisation is extremely complex and informal. For example, the National Federation of Building Trades Employers was found to have ten Regional Federations and over 260 separate Local Associations. Informality of organisation was apparent by the absence of any clear structure of hierarchical authority and disciplinary procedures in the vast majority of employers' associations.

The British employers' historical role in the development of the regulation of industrial relations has been, then, in comparison with their Scandinavian counterparts, a passive one. Britain's industrial structure, especially in the nineteenth and early twentieth centuries, the role of state intervention in wartime, industrial crises and, more recently, the various attempts of governments to control incomes have produced relatively weak employers' associations which, as the Donovan Report remarked, exhibit many traits of another 'traditional' institution – the gentlemen's club ([1] p. 144).

Despite the fragmentation of trade unionism along political and religious lines in many European countries it has been remarked that :

> all in all, there is no other trade union movement with so complex a structure as that of the British movement. ([1] p. 57)

The major feature of this generally recognised structural complexity has been the coexistence of three kinds of unionism in the system – craft, industrial and general. Many societies have two kinds of unions and a few even all three, but Britain is unique in having very powerful unions in each of the three categories.

The complexity which results from the coexistence of the three types and their relative autonomy and power is, in a very unambiguous way, a direct consequence of the early development of Britain's particular industrial infrastructure. The first successful form of union organisation were the local single craft societies which grew out of the dispersed, differentiated and 'primitive' industrial structure of the mid-nineteenth century. The subsequent introduction of mass production and the reduced dispersion of industry has obviously affected, but not eradicated, the highly decentralised structure of nineteenth-century craft unionism. On the one hand, many local societies amalgamated into federal craft unions in such industries as textiles, but they retained a great deal of autonomy. On the other hand, it has been more common for local craft unions to merge and, thereby, form branches of national multi-craft unions such as the Amalgamated Engineering Union. More recently many of the larger national craft unions have begun to admit semi-skilled workers and sometimes women, but, despite this 'dilution', the craft principle is still strongly preserved within the unions and British industry as a whole. As we have noted, this situation contrasts sharply with that in the Scandinavian countries : here the later development of industrialisation precluded the emergence of powerful and autonomous craft unions. The strength of craft unionism in Britain accounts, to a large degree, for the comparative failure of industrial unionism in Britain during the period 1890–1914. The craft groups were powerful enough to prevent the degree of coverage of an industry that the new unions were attempting to secure. Furthermore, the loose organisation of British employers and their lack of commitment to collective bargaining along industrial lines meant that, in contrast to the Swedish case, they could not become the allies of industrial against craft unionism.

The importance of general unions in Great Britain in their roles of being 'residual' and labourers' unions is clearly a consequence of the prior existence of the powerful craft and growing industrial unions. Simply, the existence of exclusive craft unions and the weakness of industry-wide bargaining, especially before 1914, encouraged the growth of unions such as the London Dockers, Gas Workers, National Amalgamated Labourers' Union, etc., which later merged into the two very large unions of Transport and General Workers' Union and General and Municipal Workers' Union.

This structural complexity of British trade unionism has also been quite closely related to the existence of a relatively weak central body. In contrast to the position in Scandinavia, the British Trades Union Congress has in the past and continues at present to have little authority over its constituent members. Two basic and interrelated reasons may be adduced for its weak position. First, by the time the T.U.C. came into existence in 1868 the many craft societies which existed were, in contrast to the Swedish case, financially secure and large enough not to require the support of a large central body. Consequently, the unions from the earliest days were careful to restrict the T.U.C.'s role to that of being the political spokesman for the labour movement. Second, in the absence of a solidary, centralised and aggressive employers' association there was little perceived need for the kind of union co-ordination that occurred in Scandinavia.[14] That is to say, even the very restricted role the T.U.C. has played developed through its relationships with governments and not the employers. Indeed, such was the early weakness of the T.U.C. that during and immediately after the First World War it was replaced by the Triple Alliance of miners, dockers and railwaymen as the major central union organisation.

Changes in the infrastructure of industry and the spurs to centralisation and normative regulation provided by two World Wars have led to changes in the institutional structure of trade unionism in the twentieth century which parallel those which we noted had occurred, for similar reasons, among the employers. First, there has been a steady and marked decline in the number of trade unions from 1425 in 1920 to 550 in 1968. This reduction is mainly a consequence of amalgamations and 'deaths' within the craft group. Second, the T.U.C. has secured its position as the formal central representative of the British labour movement, but it must be stressed that :

After 100 years, the power situation of the T.U.C. in one respect has remained almost unchanged. Neither the General

[14] There are undoubtedly other lines of development which are relevant in explaining the differences in power between the T.U.C. and the L.O. For example, the present study neglects the relationship between the trade unions and political parties. Further research may show this to be extremely important. Blake ('Swedish Trade Unions and the Social Democratic Party', *The Scandinavian Economic History Review* VIII, 1 (1960)) points out that, in Sweden, the working-class political party was formed before the central union body in contrast to Great Britain where the T.U.C. pre-dates the formation of the Labour Party by some thirty years. Moreover, he implies that the centralisation of the labour movement may have been facilitated by the prior existence of a national political party: e.g. 'Party district executives as central organizations for union activities . . . it was to them that the local unions and to some extent even the weaker national unions looked for council and support. . . .' (p. 26)

Council nor the Congress has the power to compel unions to take a particular course of action.[15]

(b) *The present system of regulation*

The extreme diversity in the normative structure of the British system of collective bargaining almost renders brief description impossible. Perhaps the only completely general statement one can make is that, in comparison with Scandinavia, Britain's industrial relations are characterised by the absence of a comprehensive and relatively uniform system of both the procedural and substantive kind which is aimed at linking local, industrial and national levels of bargaining. This diversity may be illustrated by pointing to three features of the British system : (i) the fragmentation of the normative system at the 'industry' level; (ii) the presence of 'custom' rather than formal norms at the local level; (iii) the emergence of new forms of bargaining – such as 'productivity agreements' – which are only loosely related to the traditional system.

First, although the institutionalisation of industrial relations in Britain is most developed at the 'industry' level, even here its normative structure is marked by extreme internal differentiation and diversity. There is within any one industry a variety of agreements due to the existence of a large number and types of trade unions. In some industries a single employers' association may have to conclude quite distinct agreements with 'craft', 'industrial' and 'general' unions. Similarly, unions frequently negotiate with more than one employers' association; for example, shipbuilding and engineering contain unions in common but the Shipbuilding Employers' Federation and the Engineering Employers have separate agreements with the Amalgamated Engineering Union. In addition to extreme diversity, industry-wide regulation is also very general and minimal in character. that is to say, such agreements as exist at this level necessarily lack detailed and comprehensive norms due to the extreme structural

[15] V. L. Allen, 'The Centenary of the British Trades Union Congress, 1868–1968', in *The Socialist Register*, ed. Ralph Miliband and John Saville (London, 1968) pp. 231–51.

diversity of situations to which they apply. In other words, collectively bargained agreements in Britain have traditionally been 'open-ended' and due to this low level of specificity and formalisation conflicts have tended to be, in Kahn-Freund's terms, conflicts of 'interest' rather than conflicts of 'rights'.[16]

The second characteristic feature of the traditional British system has been the existence of informal or custom-based norms for the regulation of plant-level industrial relations. The Donovan Report clearly established that, although the unions and employers' associations were involved in industry-wide negotiations, they both granted freedom to shop stewards and individual firms in local or plant bargaining. Consequently, local and unrelated agreements have proliferated in response to the relative strengths and weaknesses of employers and workers at the point of production. Moreover, in written evidence to the Royal Commission McCarthy made observations which are entirely in accord with the major arguments put forward in the present essay. It was concluded that, despite many public utterances to the contrary by prominent figures in British industry, a large proportion of managers expressed a preference for informal bargaining with shop stewards and not the official trade union officer. During their interviews with managers they uncovered a number of closely related reasons for these orientations to local bargaining. Many customary practices were viewed as managerial concessions which employers were reluctant to see become institutionalised rights and, if this were to occur, it was feared future generations of shop stewards might use such rights as a basis for more demands. Also :

some *de facto* concessions could not be written down because management, particularly at board level, would not be prepared to admit publicly that they had been forced to accept such modifications in their managerial prerogatives and formal chains of command.[17]

[16] O. Kahn-Freund, *Labour and the Law* (London, 1952) p. 58.
[17] W. E. J. McCarthy, 'The Role of Shop Stewards in British Industrial Relations', Research Paper 1, *Royal Commission on Trade Unions and Employers' Associations* (London, 1966).

Third, new forms of bargaining have emerged alongside the other two and although they may set the pattern for future developments, at the moment they merely add to the diversity of the system. Throughout the 1960s an increasing number of companies began to draw up formal plant agreements with the unions. The initiative for this type of regulation came from employers in modern large-scale continuous-process industries for whom the vagaries and unpredictability of custom-based bargaining were potentially too disruptive of their relatively long cycles of production. Such agreements often take the form of 'productivity deals' in which pay and productivity are closely related in fixed-term (usually three-year) contracts.[18] As we have already noted, it is of extreme significance that the early impetus for this kind of agreement came from companies which were outside the dominant institutions of British industrial relations. Only very slowly have British employers begun to support such types of bargaining, which are, of course, often in conflict with both the procedural and substantive elements of industry-wide bargaining. Moreover, there are signs that the pace of development in this area is slackening. During 1971–2 the engineering unions attempted to abandon industry-wide agreements in the anticipation of large wage increases at plant and company levels. The shop stewards put in claims to 2493 of the 4841 firms in the Engineering Employers' Federation, but only 1473 agreements were made and the unions have resumed negotiations with the federated employers.

Quite simply, then, the British system of industrial relations has displayed historically – and continues to do so today – an overall low level of formal normative regulation in addition to a diversity of different normative systems. Moreover, in general terms, this accounts for the absence of any 'withering away' of the strike of the kind we have observed in the Scandinavian countries. In the first place, the low level of institutionalisation means that the commonplace and recurrent conflicts of capitalist society are difficult to resolve without frequent recourse to strike

[18] For a survey and analysis of these new developments in collective bargaining see R. B. McKersie and L. C. Hunter, *Pay, Productivity and Collective Bargaining* (London, 1973).

action. This is not, of course, to say that institutionalisation inevitably reduces the inherent and 'latent' conflict or that it virtually eliminates strikes. Rather, I am in agreement with Fox and Flanders that Britain's strike pattern from 1945 to the late 1960s, which was characterised by a large number of relatively short strikes, is explicable as the response of workers to changes in the economy and structure of industry which could not be regulated by the existing low level of custom-based normative control ([6]). On the one hand, industrial mergers and the rapid expansion of new and technologically complex industries often created groups of workers who could potentially disrupt a highly interdependent process of production. Inflation and the scarcity of certain types of labour encouraged feelings of relative deprivation and the subjective awareness of this potential power and the strike 'explosion' occurred. On the other hand, the miners and dockers began to reassert their traditional militancy in the face of economic and technological changes which threaten to create high unemployment in these industries. At the same time white-collar workers began to unionise at a rapid rate and, in the absence of a centrally agreed *modus vivendi* of the Scandinavian kind between the employers and unions, recognition and jurisdictional disputes were common. Second, the plurality of normative systems, which the lack of a centralised and comprehensive framework had allowed to develop, is in its own right a source of conflict and strikes. For example, the existence of productivity bargains often has the consequence of disrupting the expectations of other workers in the same locality. The Fawley Productivity Agreement had just this effect on workers in the nearby Southampton ship-repair yards.[19]

Despite my general agreement with the diagnosis of the situation by Fox and Flanders I would argue that their explanation of the breakdown of normative regulation is incomplete. They assert that the British system is one which 'can be described in terms of Durkheim's characterisation of anomie' in the sense that normative regulation has, historically, been fragmented and

[19] T. Topham, 'New Types of Bargaining' in *The Incompatibles: Trade Union Militancy and the Consensus,* ed. R. Blackburn and A. Cockburn (Harmondsworth: Penguin Books, 1967).

custom-based rather than cohesive, uniform and formal and was, therefore, unable to withstand the pressure put on it by the growth of workers' power due to the 'accelerating pace of technological, organisational and social change of the 1960s'. ([6] p. 256) However, the question they leave unanswered is why the regulation of industrial relations by 'custom' never developed into formal and institutionalised regulation at the time in the early twentieth century, when, as they rightly pointed out, this basis for 'order' in industry began to break down. The Scandinavian countries achieved this transition from 'customary' to 'formal' norms, whereas Britain did not and it is hoped that this book has gone some way towards resolving this problem. To repeat my basic argument in this respect: the nature of Britain's industrial infrastructure would appear to have inhibited the development of nation-wide, comprehensive and uniform regulation for two interrelated reasons. In the first place, such complexity, differentiation and dispersion as British industry has displayed would, under most circumstances, inhibit the successful, non-coercive implementation of a *single* normative system. In other words, those factors which gave rise to our highly differentiated and fragmented trade union structure at one and the same time gave rise to fragmented normative regulation. Second, the way in which the industrial infrastructure shaped the British employers' organisations and orientations would seem to have ruled out the possibility that formal regulation would be encouraged, supported or even imposed from this source.

Given what was perceived as a 'crisis' of industrial relations in the 1960s and the historical inability and unwillingness of the trade unions and employers to 'voluntarily' develop regulation, the Conservative Government's imposition of authoritarian controls in the shape of the Industrial Relations Act and anti-inflation measures (1972–) are easily understandable. The nature of recent government intervention in industrial relations is not merely a result of the exigencies of an increasingly planned and controlled neo-capitalist economy but also a consequence of the British capitalist's failure 'to put his own house in order' when conditions were most favourable – that is, in the 1920s. Furthermore, the present anti-inflation measures, by virtually suspending the existing system of collective bargaining, involve a reversal of the trend towards the *institutional isolation* of industrial conflict. Thus, if this 'politicisation' of industrial conflict continues, governments in Britain are likely to change the pattern of industrial conflict from that which we witnessed in the last decade. The existence of a clearly identifiable and coercive source of grievance in the form of the state will, almost inevitably, increase the size and scope of industrial disputes. In fact, there are clear signs that this may already be happening. The large and protracted strikes of, among others, miners, post-office workers, gas workers, etc., have led to a change in Britain's strike pattern in which the number of strikes has fallen since 1970 with no decline in days lost. In other words, the large-scale strike is once again becoming commonplace.

6. CONCLUSION

THE emphasis in this essay has been on only one aspect of the institutionalisation of industrial conflict; namely, the effects of infrastructural variations on this process. The implication of this selectivity that such an approach must form the *basis* for any account of the normative content of industrial relations systems is one to which I freely admit. However, it has not been my intention to imply that such institutional systems can be completely understood by reference to the infrastructures in which they are placed. For example, it was tentatively suggested that the strength of the British state contributed to the inherent organisational weakness of employers' associations which was evident in their unwillingness to unilaterally impose normative regulation on industrial relations. The point may be generalised; that is to say, in all cases of capitalist economic development, the regulation of class conflict in industry has been the outcome of particular and varied configurations of power between workers, employers *and* the state. Thus, any extension of the kind of analysis I have presented must examine the relationships between variations in the structure of capitalist 'ruling classes' and different state structures. Similarly, differences in the organisational structure and strategies of labour movements are not exclusively related to infrastructural variations, but are also a consequence of the more narrowly political organisation of the working class. Furthermore, this political organisation must be understood in terms of the structure of political institutions and the means for controlling working-class dissent which were available at the early stages of industrialisation.

Despite this deliberate one-sidedness, I believe that this book is of some general significance for the study of industrial societies and, in particular, for the debate on 'convergence'. As is well known, the classic statement of this thesis by Kerr and his associates contained the view that a convergent pattern of development could be discerned in industrial societies due to the constraints imposed by modern technological and economic systems. The most influential criticism of the thesis has been that by Goldthorpe, who argued that Kerr and others place too little emphasis on :

> other factors which may make for possible diversity, such as different national cultures or different political systems.[1]

Consequently in recent years the debate has taken the form of an increasing stress on what may be termed 'ideal' as opposed to 'material' factors. For example, in an attempt to explain certain differences between Swedish and British perceptions and attitudes towards, among other things, social stratification a recent author has echoed Goldthorpe in stating :

> It is also necessary to investigate the structure of norms in society, and in doing so, take into account the purposive action of various social groups.[2]

However, our analysis has sought to account for some differences in the social structures of Sweden and Great Britain not by reference to a disembodied 'structure of norms' or unrooted 'purposive action', but primarily in terms of significant and persistent variations in their material infrastructures.

Proponents and critics of the convergence thesis had been in accord that there are a variety of routes to 'industrialism', but, of course, have disagreed about the consequences of 'industrialism' once established. However, both groups have seriously underestimated the extent of variety in such routes and the per-

[1] John H. Goldthorpe, 'Social Stratification in Industrial Society', in Reinhard Bendix and S. M. Lipset, *Class, Status and Power*, 2nd edn (New York, 1966) p. 648.

[2] Richard Scase, ' "Industrial Man": A Reassessment with English and Swedish Data', *British Journal of Sociology* (1972).

sistence of structural variation from this source.[3] Critics of the 'logic of industrialism' have accepted their adversaries' conceptualisation of 'industrialism', which is crude, simplistic and based almost entirely on the largest industrial systems of the West. If, as has been suggested, there are a 'variety of roads ahead' for industrial society it is not merely due to a 'diversity of values and ideologies which may underly purposive action',[4] but also because of significant diversity in exigencies posed by a variety of continuously developing material infrastructures.

[3] This is in part a consequence of maintaining too rigid a conceptual distinction between 'process' and 'structure'.
[4] Goldthorpe, op. cit., p. 659.

BIBLIOGRAPHY

THE literature which deals with the kinds of issues discussed in this essay is, unfortunately both small and inadequate. This is mainly due to the underdeveloped state of the 'sociology of industrial relations'. With few notable exceptions sociologists have neglected the 'macro' study of employer–employee relations and focused instead on 'microscopic' plant sociology.

[1] Clegg, H. A., *The System of Industrial Relations in Great Britain* (Oxford : Blackwell, 1970). The standard text, but largely atheoretical.

[2] Dahrendorf, Ralf, *Class and Class Conflict in Industrial Society* (London : Routledge & Kegan Paul, 1959) contains his views on the institutional isolation of industrial conflict.

[3] Dunlop, J. T., *Industrial Relations Systems* (New York : Holt, Rinehart, Winston, 1958). An important but neglected book which attempts to relate industrial relations systems to the economic and political structures of society.

[4] Eldridge, J. E. T., *Industrial Disputes: Essays in the Sociology of Industrial Relations* (London : Routledge & Kegan Paul, 1968) contains a review of the various theoretical approaches to the explanation of strikes.

[5] Fox, Alan, *A Sociology of Work in Industry* (London : Collier-Macmillan, 1971) contains a theoretical discussion of 'conflict and joint regulation'. Overstresses values and norms at the expense of material exigencies.

[6] Fox, Alan, and Flanders, A., 'The Reform of Collective

Bargaining : From Donovan to Durkheim', *British Journal of Industrial Relations*, VII (1969). A welcome injection of sociological theorising into the field of 'industrial relations'; like Durkheim, their account of the conditions leading to 'anomie' is incomplete.

[7] Fulcher, James, 'Class Conflict in Sweden,' *Sociology*, VII (1973). An excellent account of the structure of industrial conflict in Sweden. Contains recent Swedish data, but possibly tends to exaggerate the extent and intensity of overt conflict.

[8] Galenson, Walter, *Labor in Norway* (Cambridge, Mass. : Harvard University Press, 1949).

[9] Galenson, Walter, *The Danish System of Labor Relations* Cambridge, Mass. : Harvard University Press, 1952). Very much out of date, but the standard texts on these societies up to the Second World War.

[10] Galenson, Walter (ed.), *Comparative Labor Movements* (Englewood Cliffs, N.J. : Prentice-Hall, 1952).

[11] Högström, Gunnar, 'Recent Trends in Collective Bargaining in Sweden', *International Labour Review*, CVII (March 1973). A factual survey by a leading figure in the S.A.F.

[12] Hyman, Richard, *Strikes* (London : Fontana Books, 1972). A short account which is wider than its title suggests. Discusses the institutionalisation of industrial conflict.

[13] Johnston, T. L., *Collective Bargaining in Sweden* (London : Allen & Unwin, 1962). The standard account in English of the structure and development of the Swedish system of industrial relations. Largely descriptive.

[14] Kassalow, Everett M., *Trade Unions and Industrial Relations* (New York, 1969). A recent review of developments in Europe, North America and the 'developing' nations.

[15] Lester, Richard A., 'Reflections on Collective Bargaining in Britain and Sweden', *Industrial and Labor Relations Review*, x (1956–7). One of the few commentaries which stresses the differences between these countries.

[16] Ross, Arthur M., and Hartman, Paul T., *Changing Patterns of Industrial Conflict* (New York: John Wiley, 1960).

[17] Sturmthal, A. (ed.), *Contemporary Collective Bargaining in Seven Countries* (New York: Cornell University Press, 1957).